TALENT, EQUALITY AND MERITOCRACY

AVAILABILITY AND UTILIZATION OF TALENT

PLAN EUROPE 2000

PUBLISHED UNDER THE AUSPICES OF THE
EUROPEAN CULTURAL FOUNDATION

PROJECT 1
EDUCATING MAN FOR THE
21st CENTURY

Volume 9

TALENT, EQUALITY AND MERITOCRACY

AVAILABILITY AND UTILIZATION OF TALENT

TALENT, EQUALITY AND MERITOCRACY

AVAILABILITY AND UTILIZATION OF TALENT

by

TORSTEN HUSÉN

MARTINUS NIJHOFF / THE HAGUE / 1974

This study has been realized with support of Riksbanken, Stockholm
and the European Cultural Foundation

LA
622
·P5
vol. 9

PRINTED IN THE NETHERLANDS

TABLE OF CONTENTS

PREFACE

As Chairman of the Scientific Committee of Plan Europe 2000's Education Project of the European Cultural Foundation (Amsterdam), I would like to affirm the enormous regard we hold for this study of our colleague and friend, Professor Torsten Husén.

It is unnecessary to give a formal introduction to the man responsible for the remarkable international comparative investigations which recently have been concerned with evaluating results obtained, both qualitatively and quantitatively, by the different levels and forms of the most characteristic educational systems in the world. Through research and investigation in his native country of Sweden, primarily on a group of young men up to the time of their enlistment, Torsten Husén has illuminated the relationship between intelligence, a concept which he has shown in all its ambiguity, and the social environment. This eminent scientist has played a vital part in the reforms which have made Sweden a forerunner in developing a comprehensive and coherent system of education.

It was therefore natural that our Scientific Committee asked Professor Husén to undertake a study on a key concern of the Plan Europe 2000: the investigation of the "pool of talent".

We do not wish, at this moment, to anticipate the results of this study. It is sufficient to note that thanks to extensive research and knowledge of an interdisciplinary field which encompasses genetics, demography, experimental psychology, pedagogy, social economics and sociology, and to the author's remarkable aptitude for dealing with the concepts involved, this study answers difficult and ambiguous questions with extreme clarity and insight.

Torsten Husén unravels the complicated web of the respective influence of inherited and acquired characteristics; of the tension between equality and meritocracy; of the apparent contradiction between universal education and effective education; of the incompatibility between individual aspirations and the needs of the present system of division of labour and the labour market; and of the dialectic between the existing talent (is it a genetic given or a process with potential to develop?) and the growing intellectual demands of a "post-industrial" society. In his investigation, Torsten Husén emphasizes a long term perspective which will allow man and the social organizations which grow out of his collective consciousness, to control in some manner the "history of the future".

In this respect, the author seems to reaffirm a fundamental principle of our Plan: the development of a democracy which is enlightened, responsive and responsible, a democracy which is the safeguard of the time to come.

HENRI JANNE

FOREWORD

This book represents a long-standing research interest of mine – the study of conditions under which scholastic talent is developed and not developed. It began in 1944 when for a number of successive years I had access to test data and school records for almost complete age groups of 20-year-old men who had registered for military service. In analyzing these data it occurred to me that these data could be used in estimating the intellectual requirements at various levels of formal schooling. For some years I had the opportunity to conduct several surveys which basically aimed at finding out not only how many young people seemed to possess the ability which met the requirement of further schooling but also – and more important – how many with sufficient ability did for various reasons *not* proceed to upper secondary and university education. The latter group was at that time referred to as the "reserve of ability". For reasons spelled out in this book, particularly the growing realization in the 1950's that the supply of talent was crucial for the national economy in securing a proper growth rate, both national and international surveys began to be conducted. My own research endeavors, however, were until the end of the 1960's pursued in other directions because of my association with the Swedish school reforms. My book on *Talent, Opportunity and Career* (1969) marked a return to previous interests.

The "ability dimension" is of growing importance in our society and can be expected to become crucial in the post-industrial society. Therefore, it is indeed a highly challenging task to look at the problem of availability of talent and its utilization under a long-term perspective. This is a formidable task, because one is confronted with the whole gamut of basic problems, such as the heredity-environment issue, what should be meant by talent, how social class differences in test scores and school achievements should be interpreted, and the problem of equality versus meritocracy. I do not for a moment pretend to have dealt with any of these problems in depth. Very few of them, such as the very concept of talent and the secular trend in the development of the pool of talent, have been dealt with at some depth. Others have been brought up solely for the purpose of providing a setting for the central theme, namely the size of the pool of talent and its proper utilization in society of today and tomorrow. But by focusing on the problem of how talent is recognized and utilized in our society I have tried to bring out some of the implications of the research related to the more basic problems indicated above.

Some policy implications of the research on the utilization of the pool of talent are developed in a final chapter. It is, indeed, appropriate in concluding a study within the framework of Plan Europe 2000 to point out that these implications pertain to future educational policy. It would also be in place to emphasize that the ensuing recommendations are based on certain value premises expressed in long-term social objectives. The ones underlying the present study can be subsumed under two headings: equality of opportunity and flexibility of educational structures.

This book might never have been written had it not been for the support and amicable prodding by several persons. Professor Henri Janne, Chairman of the Scientific Committee of the Education Project, Dr. R. Georis, Secretary-General of the European Cultural Foundation and Dr. Ladislav Cerych, Director of the Education Project, have kept reminding me and have in various ways facilitated my work. Professor Torgny Segerstedt, Chairman of the Swedish Social Science Research Council and member of the Scientific Committee of the Education Project has been instrumental in securing financial support for the study.

An invitation to spend the academic year 1973–74 at the Center for Advanced Study in the Behavioral Sciences, Stanford, which meant "repeating the grade", gave me the sanctuary needed to do the reading and writing connected with the preparation of this book. I am deeply indebted to the Center for that opportunity. My wife Ingrid Husén in various ways assisted me in making the "think-tank" year productive.

I am deeply indebted to Miriam Gallaher for her careful editing. She not only removed the vestiges of my "Swenglish", but also subjected the manuscript to incisive scrutiny with regard to its logical consistency. Nancy Helmi helped me in typing two versions of the manuscript.

I am also indebted to Professors C. Arnold Anderson of the University of Chicago and Bernard Davis of Harvard University who subjected my manuscript to a critical examination, the former from the point of view of a sociologist and comparative educationalist, the latter from the point of view of a geneticist. There were many things pertaining to both structure and substance that they did not like and therefore suggested either revisions or deletions. But there were quite a few cases when I did not agree, not least because of differences in basic views. These cases are many enough in order to justify a disclaimer that these colleagues of mine should by no means be held responsible for the shortcomings that were finally sent to the printer.

TORSTEN HUSÉN

CHAPTER 1

INTRODUCTION

The tremendous change that has taken place in the Western world from a subsistence economy, then to an economy dominated by mass manufacturing of goods, and now to a post-industrial service economy has been accompanied by an equally dramatic change in the requirements placed on human beings, both in their work roles and in their roles as members of the social system at large. In a static society dominated by agriculture and handicrafts the family is the center of production and consumption, of work and leisure. It was also the major agent in preparing young people for their future roles as adults and in transferring the culture from one generation to the next. In societies in the first stage of industrialization, educational agents outside the family play a limited role in imparting certain basic skills, such as reading and writing. In most cases this agent is the elementary school, and for the great mass of people its preparatory function is completed before puberty.

But with rising expectations in regard to the role of education in preparing the young, school education has become more and more an instrument for teaching children and adolescents how to cope with new demands envisaged for them in the future. The problem, however, is that all this takes place in a rapidly changing society where the specific emerging requirements that are to be translated into specific pieces of knowledge and coping skills can scarcely be predicted. Education therefore has to prepare for a wide repertoire of unforeseen situations as well as to retrain or reeducate adults in order to facilitate their coping. We no longer live in a society where for most citizens a relatively brief period of formal preparation during childhood and adolescence will suffice. The changes connected with the advent of the post-industrial society have thrown us headlong into what is often referred to as the learning society (Husén, 1971 and 1974). In a society which, regardless of whether it has a capitalist or a socialist economy, has become progressively meritocratic, everybody needs, or at least feels he is expected, to learn up to his optimum. Economic development is conceived of as being determined by optimum utilization of human talent. Therefore the equality-meritocracy dilemma is one of the major themes of this book.

But the ability to learn, most frequently referred to as scholastic aptitude, varies considerably among individuals by the time they begin formal schooling. There has been a lively debate, reflecting controversial philosophies about human nature, as to the explanation for these differences. Most informed persons agree that the observed variability is conditioned by both genetic and environmental factors. How much variance should be attributed to the one or to the other set of factors has been a source of long-standing controversy in differential psychology and it has become particularly spirited in recent years (see, e.g., Anastasi, 1958; Hunt, 1961; Butcher, 1968; Herrnstein, 1973; Jensen, 1973). Apart from differences of opinions as to the relative roles of heredity and milieu, the great majority of scientists involved in this discussion agree that each individual is born with a genetically conditioned intelligence or talent and that the educative environment, including formal school learning, has to operate within the margin set by these hereditary conditions. On the basis of research on monozygotic (identical) twins brought up apart and on children brought up in foster homes, the margin within which the environmental factors can operate has generally been conceived of as rather narrow. However, Bereiter (1970) has pointed out that substantial differences in IQ can be attributable to environmental differences even with such a high index of heritability as 80 per cent.

But if the biologically given talent, be it general or specialized, is limited, then procedures for discovering and developing this resource become imperative in a society that has to attend to a rapidly growing technology based on both the natural and the social sciences. Advanced formal education and vocational training is no longer the privilege of an ascriptive élite but has to be given to as many as possible. In such a society "talent hunting" becomes a top priority for educational policy makers.

The post-war expansion in science and technology in the United States led the four American national research councils to appoint a Commission on Human Resources and Advanced Training, which sponsored a nation-wide survey reported in *America's Resources of*

Specialized Talent (Wolfle, 1954). The concern in the United States to keep up with the Soviet Union in terms of science and technology spurred the passing of the National Defense Education Act in 1958. The "search for talent" became suddenly a major target of research in a country with a strong egalitarian and populist tradition (CEEB, 1960).

But, obviously, the promotion of talent is not only a matter of enhancing national development and of strengthening its competitive power in economic and technological, not to speak of military, affairs. It is also a matter of enhancing the life-chances of the individual, of seeing to it that his self-realization is promoted by enriching experiences. It would therefore be appropriate right at the beginning of this book to raise the question: Talent to be utilized for what individual and social pursuits? A satisfactory answer would have to be multifaceted, and sought by analyzing socio-cultural dimensions of the concept of "talent" and of the emerging meritocratic features of the post-industrial society.

The purposes for which talent is to be utilized could be of two kinds, individual and social, two competing principles which now underlie the educational systems of Western Europe. Emphasis has been put on either the one or the other, depending upon the political and social philosophy which under certain historic and social conditions has the strongest backing in a particular country. Whereas classical liberalism placed the emphasis mainly on individual self-realization, the modern states with their strong "planning systems" (Galbraith, 1973) both in the formally public and in the private sectors tend to put more stress on the use of talent for the national economy. It is striking to note that most inquiries into the size and utilization of the pool of talent have been inspired by national concerns about the proper use of talent in promoting economic growth and social development in general.

In Europe during the 1960's, not least under the auspices of the Organization for Economic Cooperation and Development, the problem of looking out for talent took on another facet. It began to be conceived within the framework of a consistent philosophy of equality of educational opportunity. The objective became something more than providing the nation with enough highly talented and educated people to promote research and development and to man the other intellectually demanding jobs. Equality of opportunity was not limited to detection and promotion of highly talented young people in all walks of life who were supposed to "make it" on the educational ladder to the top, but was concerned as well with those who had to start from a socially underprivileged or disadvantaged level and who without the support of society would not be able to get into the "mainstream".

Both these problems – that of seeking out and fostering the potentially highly talented and that of aiding those from underprivileged backgrounds irrespective of innate talent – had already been taken up in the United States, both in the policy debate and, certainly, in social research. In America, with its populist movement and its traditional belief in the efficacy of public education provided equally to *all* children, the question of proper utilization of talent did not become a great public issue until the 1950's, when mass secondary education was already a fact and when the country was approaching the next stage of development, that of mass higher education. The issue led to vehement clashes between the élitist philosophies of individuals like Hyman Rickover (*Education and Freedom*) and Arthur Bestor (*Educational Wasteland*) and the populist and egalitarian tradition ingrained among American teachers. During the next decade, under the auspices of the Civil Rights movement and school desegregation legislation, the debate focused on the plight of ethnic minorities and the socially and economically underprivileged. Equality of educational opportunity became the main issue, epitomized by the so-called Coleman Report in 1966 and the ensuing debate.

It would, however, be wrong to say that Western Europe on the whole has been lagging behind. As a matter of fact, research on the "reserve of ability" and the ensuing methodological debates have been chiefly European endeavors inspired by the demands for extending opportunities for academic secondary education to lower class children. Shortly after the Second World War government committees were appointed in several countries with the charge of reforming the structure of the educational system. In Sweden and England, for example, these committees commissioned surveys, of which *Early Leaving* (HMSO, 1954) and the Commission on Student Aid in Sweden (SOU, 1948a) can be cited as examples. Surveys of school careers as related to home background revealed striking participation imbalances among the social strata. Typically, less than 10 per cent of the pupils who passed the examination from the academic secondary school and qualified for university entrance were of working class background. Since that social stratum represented about half the populace, this meant that in a country where about 5 percent of the relevant age group went to the university, only some 1 or 2 per cent of young people from working-class families entered the university. Several studies on the "reserve of ability" in Sweden were inspired by reforms which aimed at broadening access to upper secondary education and the university. The 1946 School Commission in its main report (SOU, 1948b) recommended undifferentiated education for the first six years of the mandatory schooling and rejected selection for an academic program at the age of 11, not because this would better take care of the more able pupils but to protect the lower classes from losing their potential spokesmen who would probably prefer the prestigious academic to the vocational program.

Attempts by futurologists within the framework of the project Plan Europe 2000 to envisage what West European society will look like by the year 2000 (Jensen *et al.*, 1972) have again brought to our attention what many social philosophers and policy makers feel to be an overriding problem: To what extent will it be possible in the next few decades to man the rapidly increasing positions – both those that can be defined in terms of relatively clear-cut professional roles and the immense number of highly demanding technical ones – with sufficiently competent people? Will the existing "inherited capital of ability" suffice, even if we devise all kinds of learning devices to develop that capital to its optimum yield? Is the post-industrial society running the risk of falling apart simply because of lack of competent manpower? Will a limited and/or badly utilized pool of talent set a low ceiling to the development of a society increasingly dependent upon a complicated technology?

The answers to these questions depend of course upon the outcome of an examination of the notion of a once-and-for-all given and fixed capital of inherited intelligence. The validity of the proposition of a fixed ceiling is closely linked to the one that learning, which in its effect makes people more competent, has to operate within a rather narrow margin. Some 25 years ago findings from intelligence surveys conducted in Europe on school children suggested a negative correlation between family size and the IQ's of the children. This was interpreted to imply that there was a long-term trend downwards in the development of the inherited intelligence, a deterioration of the gene pool. Most of this research proceeded on the assumption that the conventional intelligence tests on the whole measured "true", that is, genetically given, intelligence. Repeated testings of comparable age groups after an interval of a decade or more gave results contrary to the forecasts: the mean performance had gone up instead of down. The interpretations of these findings were legion and differed sharply according to the basic conception (with its value ramifications) of the researcher.

A major part of this book will be devoted to an examination of the proposition of the "fixed capital" of talent. This means, then, that we shall not only have to discuss the social implications of the concept of talent but also consider some important aspects of the heredity-environment issue. Two articles, a long one by Jensen (1969) in a scholarly journal and one by Herrnstein (1971) in a magazine, have elicited an avalanche of discussion that would require an entire book to review adequately. A similar debate erupted in England where Eysenck (1971) in the Galton-Burtian tradition supported the heredi-tarian views on social class differences taken by Jensen and Herrn-stein. The polarization on the heredity-environment issue has become so intense in the United States, because of its implications of racial differences with regard to intelligence and educability, that a dialogue between sociologically oriented and biologically oriented scholars has been very difficult to establish (Edmonds *et al.*, 1973). The issue whether and to what extent there are inherited social class differences in IQ has intense political implications (Edmonds and Moore, 1973). Dobzhansky (1973) and Eckland (1967) seem to be exceptions with their attempts to achieve a convergence between sociological and genetical principles. How can we make indisputable genetic diversity compatible with the overriding principle of greater social and economic equality, including equality of educational opportunity?

An extensive research since the 1940's has been conducted in Western Europe on the size of the "pool of talent" and what oppor-tunities in the educational system are open to young people, that is, how large the "reserve" of talent might be in a given country and in what social strata it can be found. It is evidently of great importance, irrespective of whether one takes a more heriditarian or a more envi-ronmental view of the availability of talent in our society, to find out to what extent the measure of observed talent is developed at the various levels of the educational system. This is what Wolfle (1954), for instance, did in the United States and the present author did when he conducted his surveys in Sweden in the 1940's. The debate triggered by these and other studies has made it possible to tackle the problems of talent utilization today with a good deal more precise conceptuali-zation and methodological sophistication.

The constraints on the utilization of observed talent are legion and deserve to be dealt with in a separate chapter. The structure of a system can in itself serve as a constraint by rigidly channeling pupils into specific types of schools or tracks within schools. The earlier this takes place the more pronounced are the differences between social strata in participation in further education. Grade-repeating is a practice which serves selective purposes not only according to objective scholastic criteria but also with regard to social background. A "streaming" of pupils essentially has the same effect. The content of the curriculum and teaching practices can be biased against certain groups of pupils. Thus, the large sex difference in, for instance, Science can to a considerable extent be regarded as an outcome of a curriculum which is geared to the needs of a male-oriented society.

The hopes for education as a "great equalizer" have been high in both capitalist and socialist economies. Improved education has been conceived to be a "spearhead toward the future" and to raise the level of employability of the poor and hitherto disadvantaged and thereby to enhance their life chances. Therefore, by making massive educational resources available to education one would not only boost the economic level of the individual and society at large but also solve major social problems, such as that of mass poverty. This conception is, at least partly, reflected in the title of a book by Harbison (1973), *Human Resources as the Wealth of Nations*. Since the 1950's many economists have supported this conception of a rate-of-return theory, according to which education produces as much return as investment in physical capital and can strongly affect the income distribution in society. This also reflects a theory of "wage competition" which assumes supply-and-demand mechanisms.

Notions about the return of education *per se* have in recent years been challenged by both economists and other social scientists. GNP has over a long period gone up much more slowly than investment in education. Income differentials between holders of occupations at various levels of education have increased instead of decreased, as in, for instance, the United States, where the tremendous increase of formal education has been concomitant with widening gaps of earnings between the various education categories (Jencks, 1972).

Researchers, particularly those with a Marxian view on social problems, have challenged the notion that general rise in either IQ or education is conducive to economic success. Thus, Jencks (1972) in his book on *Inequality* points out that the correlation between background and career has not changed significantly over the last few decades which could be interpreted as an indication that increased fluidity in terms of social mobility has not been achieved. The interpretation of the complex and hard to disentangle relationship between social background, IQ, formal education and occupational career is, however, beset with many pitfalls (Levin, 1972; Coleman *et al.*, 1973). The contention that neither IQ nor education makes much difference in conditioning adult economic careers has to be thoroughly examined before being accepted. The research on factors conducive to social mobility by Blau and Duncan (1967) could thereby serve as a starting point. The "knowledge industry", both the part that produces and the part that distributes knowledge, will grow in the post-industrial society; that is, scientific research will expand and the time set aside for formal learning experiences provided within and outside the framework of institutional schooling will lengthen. It has been said that educated ability is the democratic substitute for inherited status and wealth. Life careers are no longer, as in a feudal society, assigned on an ascriptive basis but are expected to be "achieved" (Linton, 1936). This gives rise to the question whether there is an inherent incompatibility between democratic egalitarianism and the conditions of economic growth. The equality-meritocracy incompatibility – or at least dilemma – ought to be analyzed and made explicit. One way to do this is by scrutinizing the evidence for or against education and IQ as determiners of occupational and economic success.

The outcomes of the inquiry undertaken in this book have certain policy implications. In the first place they will have relevance for the long-term educational policy. For instance, to what extent is mass higher education a realistic prospect? How "high" can it be? The answers to such questions depend evidently upon which conclusion one arrives at: that the "pool of ability" is by and large fixed and that the "reserves" will soon become exhausted, or that the capital of ability can be increased, i.e., can be changed by social and economic policy. In terms of educational policy the dilemma is very much one of achieving a proper balance between (a) selectivity, competitiveness and the need to constantly improve oneself in the post-industrial economy against (b) the broadening of access to education, the removal of structural rigidities which reinforce selection, and the enhancement of flexibility by making it easier to reenter the educational system after having left it.

CHAPTER 2

TALENT – GENETICALLY AND/OR SOCIOLOGICALLY CONCEIVED

THE HEREDITY-ENVIRONMENT ISSUE

In the debate on the utilization of talent, whether spurred by demands for increased equity of participation or by national manpower needs, two opposing views about the availability and development of talent have been advanced. These views are at the base of quite different policies. The one, which might be called the élitist, tends to regard talent as mainly or almost entirely inherited and to interpret social class or racial differences in intelligence, school participation and occupational careers as largely caused by these differences (Jensen, 1969; Eysenck, 1973; Herrnstein, 1973). One preoccupation is to preserve the gene pool and to take such eugenic measures as to prevent the national intelligence from declining. The able pupils from the lower classes will by the inherent force of their endowment rise to the positions in society which are justified by their inherited eminence. The other view, which might be labeled the egalitarian or social reconstructivist, holds that inherited intelligence is by and large randomly distributed over social classes and regards social class differences in school participation and attainments as remnants of an unjust privilege society where parental prerogatives are passed on to the children. Equality of access to participation not only in education but also in social and economic matters at large will create a just society. The Marxist version is to regard competence as something conferred upon the individual by the society. In an article on the educational views of the present author in *Sovjetskaja Pedagogica*, J. M. Sokolov (1970) comments upon the research conducted on the "pool of ability" in Sweden in the following way: "As in the past, some bourgeois researchers even today conceive of human ability as an individual psychological function. Such a view reflects the interest of the exploiting classes. Maintaining that individual success in life is directly dependent upon the individual's subjective assets and not upon the socio-economic conditions is an easy method of diverting the attention of the working masses from the real causes of socio-economic and cultural inequality under capitalism."

But regardless of whether and to what degree they were adherents of the élitist or the egalitarian view, most of those involved in the debate on the proper utilization of the pool of talent have assumed (although in most cases tacitly) that "talent" is determined mainly by a given, and therefore limited, pool of genes. The mere fact that the phrase "reserve of ability" was coined by a radical reformer and was for a long time generally accepted indicates that the view of a genetically fixed pool of talent prevailed well into the last decade. Halsey (1961) was an early exception by pointing out the misleading implications of the metaphor. It was conducive to the idea that "talent" could not be increased by steps taken within the educational system or by welfare policy. The main policy action therefore seemed to be to see to it that those with enough inherited talent could get access to educational institutions that could adequately develop their capacities. In a paper submitted to the Robbins Committee Vernon (1963) challenged the view "that there exists in the population a fixed distribution or 'pool' of intelligence, which limits either the number of individuals capable of higher education, or the educational standards that can be achieved by groups of pupils and students of given IQ level" (p. 45).

The history of the changing concept of intelligence has been written by Hunt (1961, 1969). In the Preface to his 1961 monograph on "Intelligence and Experience" he makes the following statement:

"For over half a century, the leading theory of man's nature has been dominated by the assumptions of fixed intelligence and predetermined development. These beliefs have played a large role in psychological theorizing and investigations; they have provided a conceptual framework for the measurement of intelligence and for accounting for the development of human abilities, which have been regarded as the unfolding of capacities almost completely determined by inheritance. Recently, however, a transformation has been taking place in this traditional conception of intelligence and its relationship to experience. Evidence from various sources has been forcing a recognition of central processes in intelligence and of the crucial role of life experience in the development of these central processes" (Hunt, 1961, p. V).

In a recent presentation, where he develops his thinking on the bearing of the heredity-environment issue on social class and ethnic differences, Hunt (1973) has brought his thought on this matter up to date.

Cyril Burt in England has been the most prominent proponent of the Galton tradition of "hereditary genius" which was part of the more comprehensive theory of natural selection according to which certain important human traits are genetically fixed. Galton, inspired by his interest in mental inheritance, proposed to the Anthropological Section of the British Association for the Advancement of Science a survey on mental capacities. Burt together with among others Spearman and McDougall was assigned to construct the tests (Burt, 1972). In one of his latest publications Burt (1969) defined intelligence as "innate, general, cognitive ability". Apart from the impact of the Darwin-Galton tradition Burt's views carried heavy weight since he once pioneered the massive use in British schools of intelligence tests. All his life Burt (1972) took a strong position on the side of the heredi-tarians and he also drew practical conclusions in terms of siding with the élitists against those who were proponents of a comprehensive secondary school and who wanted to abolish the eleven-plus exami-nations (Cox and Dyson, 1969). As indicated above, the hereditarian view has been closely associated with conservative policy conceptions, whereas the environmental view has been prevalent among liberals who have favored educational provisions on a broader and more equi-table basis.

In his 1973 exposition of the heredity-environment issue Hunt (*op. cit.*, p. 5) points out that defining "intelligence as an innate ability has the defect of leaving it unmeasurable", simply because what is observ-able are the test scores, the phenotype, whereas not even a dogmatic hereditarian would claim that these scores are pure measures of the genotype, the "native wit". This confusion has led to maintaining the highly artificial distinction between intelligence tests and achievement tests. Such a distinction has been made in spite of the fact that in-telligence tests have been validated against academic attainments and then referred to as "scholastic aptitude tests".

We are beginning to arrive at a consensus that the two types of tests, typical group or individual intelligence tests and achievement tests, particularly in reading and writing, differ mainly with regard to the range of experiences they tap. No distinct demarcation line be-tween them can be established. The conventional intelligence tests that have been used to measure scholastic ability are at best measures of cognitive skills, which are strategic in absorbing the learning material presented in the ordinary school situation. Many of these tests tap what Cattell (1971) has referred to as "crystallized" intelligence, skills which are necessary prerequisites for more "fluid", problem-solving operations at a "higher" mental level.

Thus, as Hunt points out, intelligence as measured by the conventional tests is to a large extent a *product* of learning not only a cause behind it. This conception has been emphasized by Ferguson (1956) who views the factors obtained from factor analyses as clusters of over-learned skills. This, certainly, makes sense for an interpretation of several of the "primary mental abilities" arrived at by Thurstone (1938). Hunt also refers to Gagné's (1968) model of a transfer hierarchy, all the way from simple S-R connections through various processes of discrimination and concept-building to problem-solving.

INTELLECTUAL GROUP DIFFERENCES

It would in this context be out of the question to survey the enormous research literature in the field of group differences in intelligence, not to mention the equally extensive and often polemic popular literature inspired by the debate on race and social class differences. The nation-wide survey commissioned by the United States Congress, which James S. Coleman and his associates published in 1966, on equality of educational opportunity led to an intensive methodological debate relating mainly to the role played by the school as compared to social background in imparting competence in pupils (Mood, 1970; Mosteller and Moynihan, 1972). The genetic aspect was completely left out of the debate, and in the multivariate analyses "native wit" was tacitly included among the background factors. In the 1960's the Project Headstart was launched on the basis of the "deprivation hypothesis". The dismal academic performances of Black children were, according to this hypothesis, due mainly to the social and cultural deprivation under which they had lived up to the time of entering school. Headstart was supposed to partly make up for the deficit by providing stimulating experiences and imparting cognitive skills that would make it easier for the deprived children to get into the academic "mainstream". After a few years, however, misgivings, based partly on attempts to evaluate the outcomes of the project (Hughes and Hughes, 1972), had begun to be aired as to the worthwhileness of the program. Furor broke loose when Jensen in a celebrated article in the

Harvard Educational Review challenged the main assumption upon which the project was built (Jensen, 1969). The introductory sentence has become famous: "Compensatory education has been tried and it apparently has failed" (*op. cit.*, p. 2).

The reason given for the failure was mainly the following. The "social deprivation" or "average child" hypothesis – i.e. that all children basically are alike, but some fail at school because they have been socially disadvantaged – is wrong. The "allied belief that those children of ethnic minorities and the economically poor who achieve 'below average' in school do so mainly because they begin school lacking certain crucial experiences which are prerequisites for school learning" (*op. cit.*, p. 4) is also wrong, since "compensatory" or "enrichment" programs had yielded results far below expectations. Cognitive competence, as measure by IQ, was supposed to be boosted by these programs. "So here is where our diagnosis should begin – with the concept of the IQ: how it came to be what it is; what it 'really' is; what makes it vary from one individual to another; what can change it, and by what amount" (*op. cit.*, p. 5).

Thus, the entire 123-page article makes an attempt to evaluate the vast literature on individual differences in IQ and how these are affected by genetic and environmental influences. A group of psychologists invited by the journal to present their views were on the whole highly critical of the firm genetic view taken by Jensen in accounting for ethnic differences in IQ and scholastic achievement (HER, 1969a, 1969b).

The acerbated discussion in the United States has, of course, to be viewed in the context of the Civil Rights legislation and attempts to achieve more equity in life chances as between Blacks and Whites. But the arguments that Jensen advances apply with as much force to social class as to racial differences. This explains why an article in *Atlantic Monthly* by psychologist Richard Herrnstein (1971) under the neutral title "IQ", where he makes a case for the modern social Darwinism that goes under the label "meritocracy", was met with such fury, in spite of the fact that no explicit reference was made to racial differences.

The Jensen *Harvard Educational Review* article plus a series of other articles by him germane to the scholarly debate that ensued have subsequently been published in a collection called *Genetics and Education* (Jensen, 1972). The Preface conveys a vivid impression of the intensive reactions that followed on the original article. A later book, *Educability and Group Differences* (Jensen, 1973), is a follow-up of the first article, where in the main emphasis was on individual differences. In the later book Jensen sets out even more explicitly to "challenge some of the prevailing explanations" of group differences, "particularly those theories that involve exclusively social and psychological causative factors" (*op. cit.*, p. 1). From the outset he acknowledges that the evidence for heritability that he presents is derived from studies of *individual* differences (twin partners, foster child – foster parent). He thinks, however, that it is highly probable that one can generalize from these findings to apply also to group differences. "Although one cannot formally generalize from *within*-group heritability to *between*-group heritability the evidence from studies of within-group heritability does, in fact, impose severe constraints on some of the most popular environmental theories of the existing racial and social class differences in educational performance." (*ibid.*)

Herrnstein (1973) has also followed up by telling the story of the furor created by his article of 1971 and elaborating on the points he made on the genetic foundation of IQ and indirectly of success in society. He reviews the research literature on intelligence, its uses, and the nature-nurture controversy, and brings out the meritocratic implications. His conclusions may best be summarized by quoting from the Preface:

"There is evidence not only for the genetic ingredients in mental capacity but also in social status. Many of the means and ends of contemporary social policy fail to take into account those biological constraints, and they may consequently misfire. Equalizing educational opportunity may have the unexpected and unwelcome effect of emphasizing the inborn intellectual differences between people. It may instead be better to diversify education. ... Even the effort to encourage social mobility may have its penalties. The biological gap between social classes will grow if the people who rise from lower to higher status are selected for their native ability ..." (*op. cit.*, p. 10).

This was the message intended for the readers of the article on "IQ". The message seemingly did not get through.

In an article reviewing some of the research Eysenck (1973) makes a case for social class differences. He cites studies on twins and foster children and arrives at the conclusion that the amount of variance accounted for by hereditary and environmental factors respectively can be set at 80 and 20 per cent. But the strongest argument in favor of the decisive influence of genetic factors on ability he finds in the well-known phenomenon of regression to the mean between generations.

He quotes from a study made by Cyril Burt on intergenerational social mobility. Only some 40 per cent of the upper class or upper middle class children end up in the same status category as their parents, while some 15 per cent of the working class children move to the upper or upper middle status. Thus, the regression mechanism in a way would be a hereditary guarantee for social mobility. In the same vein as Herrnstein (1971) Eysenck regards inherited talent as a kind of guarantee for a just society. Everybody rises – or, as the case may be, falls back – to the level of competence that is pre-established in his or her genes.

HERITABILITY

Apart from findings in more or less controlled experiments, whereby children have been subjected to changes in environment, the major part of empirical evidence upon which the recent nature-nurture debate has been based comes from twin studies (Vandenberg, 1966). Intrapair differences among identical (or monozygotic) twins reared together and apart have provided what has been regarded as key evidence. Furthermore, comparisons with regard to such differences have been made between identical and fraternal twins reared together. The other main research strategy has been to compare similarity in terms of parent-child correlation in children who are brought up with their biological parents with those who are brought up by foster parents and with similarity between child and biological parents among foster children.

Heritability is defined by the proportion of the variance within a given population in the measure of a certain characteristic which is accounted for by the genotypic variation *within the population under study*. Thus, heritability is not primarily a fixed genetic entity. It is, as Dobzhansky (1973) points out, "not an intrinsic property of a trait but of the population within which it occurs". If the population under study were to consist of individuals who are genetically identical or close to identical, then heritability would be close to zero or zero in all traits. Conversely, if all individuals live in an environment that is identical or close to identical, then heritability would be unity or close to unity. "Therefore," Dobzhansky concludes, "estimates of heritability are valid only for the populations and for the times when the data on which they are based were collected" (*op. cit.*, p. 17). This is a special case of the general principle that heredity is "not a status but a process" (*op. cit.*, p. 8). The phenotype of a certain characteristic emerges as a result of the interactive encounter between certain genes and a certain set of environmental factors. This is to say that they must covary.

The conception of heritability is, when applied to individuals, obviously beset with certain pitfalls. It reflects, as Cronbach (1973) points out, "the distribution of opportunities in a certain place and time". It is, then, "a sociohistorical fact". This limitation has certain implications. The present author has pointed out that the hereditary background of illiteracy has changed tremendously during the last centuries due to changes in opportunity to enter school (Husén, 1951a). In Europe a few hundred years ago, when the majority of the population was illiterate, this obviously was due to lack of opportunities, whereas today, when compulsory primary schooling has been instituted in these countries, heritability of skills constituting literacy would have been much lower if it had been measured.

More important, however, when it comes to the study of intrapair twin differences within pairs reared apart, are the environmental differences *within* the pairs. In practically all cases where such studies have been conducted, the partners have been adopted by parents within the same culture, with the same language and with certain similarities in terms of social status (Kamin, 1973). Thus, we have no information about what would have happened in terms of intrapair differences if the environments had been much more different from each other. In other words: the study of intrapair differences among separated identical twin partners cannot serve as a substitute for experimental or interventionist conditions where drastic measures can be taken to influence, for instance, cognitive development. Twin studies or comparisons between children and foster parents do not provide us with realistic estimations of what geneticists refer to as the "norm of reaction". As Hunt (1973) points out, they "tell us nothing of how much the IQ might be changed by newly designed systems of child-rearing and education. It is not relevant to why Project Head Start succeeded or failed" (*op. cit.*, p. 19).

The present author (Husén, 1960, 1963), who conducted studies of achievement test scores of national populations of twins at the 4th, 6th and 8th grade levels, made the observation that intraclass correlations for at least the identical pairs tended to *increase* instead of decrease in successive age groups. The opposite could be expected on the basis of the assumption that genetic and environmental factors act in an additive way independently of each other. According to the generally assumed conception observed intrapair variance consists of two variances, one genetic (s_G^2) and one environmental (s_M^2), where G stands for genetic factors and M for milieu factors. The simple formula would then be:

$$s^2 = s_G^2 + s_M^2.$$

With access to both monozygotic and dizygotic twins it would then be possible to determine the relation between s_G and s_M. We have, however, also to take into account the error of measurement (E) and thus add the error variance s_E^2 and rewrite the formula as follows:

$$s^2 = s_G^2 + s_M^2 + s_E^2.$$

Dobzhansky (1973) was quoted above as pointing out that genetic and environmental factors covary. The very fact of being genetically more alike affects the way the two partners in a monozygotic pair perceive the world and the way they react to it. Furthermore, it affects the way persons in their environment treat them. The great majority of adults, and even in many cases their parents and siblings, mistake them for each other (Husén, 1959). The monozygotic twins have a much stronger intrapair emotional attachment and are much more eager to do the same things and to be treated alike than are the dizygotic twin partners (Husén, 1959).

In a study of intrapair differences in school achievements (Husén, 1963) the present author hypothesized that a correlation due to inter-action could be assumed to operate between the G and M factors and that the formula therefore could be rewritten as follows:

$$s^2 = s_G^2 + s_M^2 + s_E^2 + r_{GM} \cdot s_G \cdot s_M.$$

Comparisons were made between two national grade cohorts of both monozygotic and dizygotic twins, from grades 4 and 6 respectively. The findings were briefly as follows. Intraclass correlations for both identical and fraternal twins went up by 10 to 15 hundreths from the age of 11 to the age of 13 for reading and writing test scores, whereas the rise for arithmetic test scores was only 5 to 6 hundreths, which was not significant for identical twins.

The interpretation offered was:

"The increase of intrapair similarity may be taken to reflect the probable existence of an interaction between genetic and environmental factors ... This would express itself in the tendency of identical

twins, by virtue of their primary likeness, to share a common environmental experience and accordingly to act alike. Conversely, fraternal
twins, by virtue of their primary unlikeness, would experience their
environment differently and accordingly tend to act increasingly
unlike. If this is so, the intraclass correlations for identical pairs ought
to increase with rising age, while those for fraternals ought to fall off
or in any event not increase" (Husén, 1963, p. 113).

Estimations of heritability are in most cases derived from studies
where similarities of co-twins among monozygotic and dizygotic twins
have been compared. Such comparisons are based upon the assumption
that the environments of the partners in a dizygotic co-twin pair is
not more dissimilar than in a co-twin monozygotic pair. Such an assumption is indeed doubtful considering the outcomes of studies of
attachment within the pairs (Husén, 1959). Scarr (1968) conducted a
study of 61 same-sex pairs (girls) of elementary school age and found
that monozygotic co-twins were treated somewhat more similar by
their parents than dizygotic co-twins. The central problem here is
whether and to what extent the greater similarity in parental treatment of monozygotic co-twins is due to greater factual similarity or
reflects expectations of greater similarity. By using pairs where the
parents were wrong about the zygosity Scarr arrived at evidence that
supported the second interpretation, i.e., that the parents, in a way,
tended to "train similarity".

It has been strongly emphasized above that indices of heritability
are derived from *specific populations* and at best apply to the *average
individual* within that population. Such an index which is derived
from *one* population cannot without strong reservations be applied to
another population.

The mere fact that heritability estimations of IQ measures are arrived
at from European-American white school populations imposes serious
limitations on their applicability. There is, indeed, meager justification
for using them in accounting for racial group differences. One could
conceive of *different* indices of heritability in different populations (e.g.
Scarr-Salapatek, 1971).

The interactive relationship between genetic and environmental
factors in a society in the process of rapid change can be illustrated as
follows. Until a few decades ago only one child out of a hundred
entered the upper secondary school in Sweden and was headed for the
matriculation examination which qualified for university entrance. In
1945 the present author (Husén, 1946) after conducting a national

survey analyzed intelligence test scores and information about formal schooling for an entire age cohort of Swedish 20-year olds being examined for conscription. On the basis of certain assumptions the proportion of an age cohort that could be assumed to be intellectually capable of passing the matriculation examination was estimated to be 13–14 per cent, which was almost three times the proportion actually taking the examination at that time. Furthermore, at about the same time Neymark (1952) in his studies on selective migration showed that some 60 per cent of the children with professional and managerial background took this examination as compared to only 1–2 per cent of those with blue-collar background. It was then maintained by the skeptics that one should not infer from this survey that the country had any considerable "reserves of ability" (Quensel, 1949). It was implied that the glaring differences between upper and lower social strata in school participation could be assumed to reflect genuine hereditary differences between the strata. Later on, the school reforms in the 1950's and 1960's, which broadened access to further education for children from working class families and rural areas, in some sense provided a test of the hypothesis of the strength of hereditary social class differences. By the end of the 1960's the enrollment in the first grade of the upper secondary school (*gymnasium*) had increased to about 30 per cent, and the proportion of the relevant age group passing the matriculation examination (which was abolished in 1968) was about 20 per cent. This was far above the estimation some 20–25 years earlier. The examination requirements had in the meantime not changed considerably. The proportion of children in the relevant age group with working class background completing the *gymnasium* had by then increased from about 2 to about 10 per cent. (sou, 1973)

Evidently, this educational growth from the middle of the 1940's to the end of the 1960's was not a change taking place in a social vacuum. It was part and parcel of the development of the country to a social welfare state. As a matter of fact, there are many indications that the school reforms reflected an increased "social demand" for education that was stimulated by the major social reforms (Paulston, 1968).

Anyhow, nobody, not even the strongest proponents of a system of comprehensive education that would broaden the opportunities for children from the lower classes to get access to advanced education, could at the middle of the 1940's imagine that 25 years later the élite school that prepared for the university would have expanded its enrollment by some 400 per cent. Those who were supposed to be *gymnasium* and/or university "material" were expected to come mainly from the class whose parents themselves had a good education, and to have thereby learned to profit from a favorable and stimulating home environment.

Ekman (1951), in a most important contribution to the research methodology on the pool of ability, which we shall deal with in more detail later (pp. 52 *et seq.*), started from the assumption that children who grew up in families belonging to professional and managerial strata obtained an optimal degree of stimulation and support needed for a successful school career. In this group one could therefore calculate at each ability level the probability for a successful passing of the matriculation examination. These probabilities could then be applied to the other social strata. In a way the advent of the social welfare society has partially established the conditions which were in a somewhat utopian way assumed in Ekman's study.

The above large-scale (uncontrolled) social "experiment" has been reported because of its bearing on the usefulness of applying heritability indices derived from one population to another population where the environmental conditions are different. What we have in mind here are comparisons between racial, ethnic, and social class populations with regard to their level of intelligence and educability. Jensen (1969, 1973) arrives at the conclusion that the differences between Blacks and Whites in both educability and IQ are due mainly to genetic differences. It does not convince him or others who have argued along the same line that heritability indices, which account for racial differences, could vary according to the degree of stimulating influences in the milieux which are typical for the respective groups.

From what has been said above the following hypothesis emerges. One could expect genetic differences to manifest themselves more markedly when the children are subjected to more stimulating and in various respects favorable environments; such differences can be expected to be more or less hampered or suppressed in environments where the circumstances are depriving and non-stimulating. "Social deprivation" or "cultural disadvantage" refers to factors associated with poverty that prevent the optimal development of certain psychological traits, be they cognitive or non-cognitive.

Findings from a study of 3,042 twins (493 opposite-sex and 1,028 same-sex pairs) in the Philadelphia school system by Scarr-Salapatek (1971) are worth mentioning here. The mean difference between Blacks and Whites in achievement was smaller (about one third of a standard deviation) among children from the lower class than among those from the middle and upper classes, where it amounted to almost one standard deviation. The spread in test scores was greater among the privileged than among the underprivileged children. These findings (which have been partly disputed by Jensen, 1973, pp. 182 *et seq.*) support the hypothesis that the heritability index tends to be greater among the privileged than among the underprivileged.

Since the Scarr-Salapatek study (in spite of the obvious drawback of not using twins whose zygosity had been diagnosed) could, as Dobzhansky (1973, p. 21) points out, be regarded as a "breakthrough in heritability studies", it is worthwhile summarizing its methodology and major findings. She advanced two competing models which she then tried to test by means of twin data collected in one big school district, Philadelphia. The first model was built on the overall hypothesis that group differences in IQ, as measured by intelligence tests, are due mainly to environmental factors; that is, certain factors such as parental education, parental economic standing, and culturally stimulating contacts account for the major portion of the group differences. If the hypothesis is valid, then the more advantaged a group is in respects relevant to IQ performances the more one can expect that group to show greater genetic and less environmental variance. The better the conditions for the development of cognitive skills the greater the likelihood that the inherited potential will be realized. This means that the genotype-phenotype correlation can be predicted to be higher in the high SES (socio-economic stratum) than in the low one.

The second model started from the overall hypothesis that genetic differences are the primary determinants of performance differences between social and racial groups living under varying conditions. The small environmental effects are then assumed to be mainly of the "threshold" type, that is, to be of little or no effect at all under a certain threshold of stimulation. The prediction is that the heritability index will be the same in different SES or racial groups.

According to the first model it was hypothesized that social class factors would affect the intrapair similarities and therefore the estimations of heritability. The lower class twins living under deprived conditions would not have the same opportunity as the middle or upper class twins to realize their potential. Thus, the genetic part of the variance of intellectual performance could be expected to be lower among lower class than among middle or upper class twins, since their intraclass correlations are expected to be reduced by the depriving social conditions.

The findings were: "In the middle to above-median SES groups, the same-sex correlations exceeded the opposite-sex correlations for all three aptitude scores in both races... For the disadvantage group, the failure of same-sex correlations to exceed opposite-sex correlations makes it doubtful that the proportion of genetic variance in the lower class group equals that of the advantaged group. Total variance was generally larger in the advantaged than in the disadvantaged groups of both races. For whites, total variance was larger in all six comparisons of advantaged and disadvantaged groups. For blacks, total variance was larger in four of six comparisons. This finding reflects the greater phenotypic variability of advantaged children, as predicted in model 1... Thus, the major finding of the analysis of variance is that advantaged and disadvantaged children differ primarily in what proportion of variance in aptitude scores can be attributed to environmental sources" (p. 1292).

Scarr-Salapatek points out important implications of these findings. Most lower class children, and the Blacks were mostly of this class, lacked the experience which is conducive to the development of scholastic skills, such as parents with good education, broad vocabularies and a school-minded attitude. The implication is that the genetic variation behind the development of what is referred to as scholastic aptitude did not have an opportunity to develop into phenotypic variation among lower class children to the same extent as among middle or upper class children. This means that school-related experiences are relatively more important to disadvantaged than to advantaged children. This turned out to be one of the more significant findings from the Coleman (1966) survey.

In his book on educability and group differences Jensen (1973) takes up the serious challenge against hereditary interpretation of racial differences in IQ and scholastic attainments that is entailed in Scarr-Salapatek's study. He rightly points out that the lack of a zygosity diagnosis and the necessity to rely on comparisons between correlations for same-sex and opposite-sex twin pairs enlarges the standard errors of the estimated within-pair correlations. But it seems that the ensuing systematic error connected with this crude method works against her hypothesis. Jensen introduces the principle of regression toward the population mean in accounting for the mean difference between black and white twins. But he overlooks, in spite of quoting Scarr-Salapatek correctly on this point, her emphasizing that one can expect different regression effects for Blacks and Whites *"if* the two races indeed have *genetically* different population means" (Jensen, *op. cit.*, p. 185, italics added). Jensen assumes that the Black population would regress downward toward its phenotypic population mean of 85 whereas the White population would regress upward toward its mean of 100. Apart from the fact that no measures are available for the population means from which the twin pairs have been drawn, it should be borne in mind that the regression that might occur varies with the *amount* of genetic influence on the phenotype. But Jensen finds that what at best can be concluded from the Scarr-Salapatek study is that the heritability tends to be lower in the lowest social class than in the middle and upper. In his view this can be regarded as support for a "threshold theory", according to which far down on the environmental scale at a certain point the summative effect of cultural and material deprivation acts as a serious suppressor to the genetic potential.

The Scarr-Salapatek study has triggered a debate (see, e.g., Allen *et al.*, 1973 and Scarr-Salapatek, 1973) which to a large extent has dealt with the degree of methodological rigor of the investigation. Allen and Pettigrew point out that the two competing models employed are set up to make simple predictions, either that favorable environments increase the mean, variability and heritability of IQ or that they do not. In her rejoinder Scarr-Salapatek quotes Tanner, whose research on environmental disadvantage supports her model: "... environmental deprivation – in this case nutritional, social, and emotional disadvantages – has a generally depressing effect on average physical growth in a total population and both a depressing and variable effect on the expression of genetic differences among individuals. A principal effect is lowered heritability of differences in physical growth in disadvantaged populations." (*op. cit.*, p. 1046) There are indications that the same applies to intellectual development.

Kamin (1973) has subjected the major studies of identical twins reared apart to a detailed scrutiny in terms of both methodology and conceptualization. The outcome is not very encouraging, notably with regard to methodological rigor. In Burt's (1966) case it is devastating, particularly in its detailed pinpointing of lack of basic information about how the data were collected and under what circumstances. Furthermore, Kamin shows that there is an appalling lack of consistency in defining and reporting from one occasion to the other. His conclusion is: "The numbers left behind by Professor Burt are simply not worthy of serious scientific attention" (p. 11). Shields (1962) in an impressive monograph presented 40 monozygotic pairs brought up apart. But from the details presented in his Appendix one learns that in 27 cases the two partners were reared in related branches of the parent's families. Only in 13 pairs were the two partners brought up in unrelated families. For these 13 cases an intraclass correlation of .51 was obtained. But since one can suspect that the milieux to some extent are correlated, even that relatively low coefficient might have been spuriously inflated. The trouble with the classical Newman-Freeman-Holzinger (N-F-H) (1937) study from the 1930's is that age-IQ correlations contribute to inflating the intraclass correlation for the pairs reared apart. The same applies to the Juel-Nielsen (1965) study. If the age effect is taken out from both the N-F-H and Juel-Nielsen studies, Kamin finds that the intraclass correlations are heavily reduced. The main snag with studies of adopted children is the selective allocation that adoption agencies employ which limits the value of heritability estimations arrived at by comparing adopted children with their adoptive parents and with their biological parents as well. The heritability estimates obtained by this method by and large are of the same order of magnitude as those arrived at by the twin method.

THE IMPLIED SOCIAL CRITERIA IN DEFINING INTELLIGENCE

Back in the 1940's the present author had the opportunity to utilize data on almost complete national age groups of 20-year-old males who had been called up for conscription, when they went through a medical and psychological examination. They completed a questionnaire on their education and occupational experiences, showed their school certificates, and had to take an intelligence test. The latter was group-administered and drew heavily on verbal material (see Husén and Henricson, 1951). The test scores were related to the amount of formal education as well as to the occupational status. In writing up a monograph titled "Ability and Environment" (Husén, 1948), the author was faced with the task of defining what he referred to as the "intelligence" or "ability" that had been measured by the group test. After having reviewed various verbal definitions he noted that all of them were beset with value judgments which had not been made explicit since the definitions were allegedly "objective". Intelligence was for instance defined as "thinking rationally", "acting adequately", and "responding efficiently". It was pointed out – something which at that time did not seem self-evident – that the behaviors from which intelligence was inferred were all assessed against some kind of value standard, which could vary from one socio-cultural context to another.

More than 20 years later, when the author undertook the task of reviewing the research pertaining to social background and educational attainment, the thesis of value standards underlying conceptions of intelligence was further developed (Husén, 1972). For if the criterion behaviour in terms of learned cognitive skills, according to which an individual's intelligence is assessed, is decisive in assigning social status or reflects a quality decisive in producing ascribed status, then social class and ethnic differences are the logical outcomes. It was pointed out in a translation from the presentation in 1948:

"Different socio-cultural settings vary in the demands they make on intelligence or, to express it more accurately, they require not only different amounts but chiefly different *kinds* of intelligence. Consequently each social context demands and trains just the variety of intelligence that is needed for that particular setting" (Husén, 1972, p. 44).

In cultures where high premium is put on manual dexterity such a trait will determine the social prestige and the life success of individuals and might eliminate group differences in certain cognitive skills. "In our modern technological and complex society, it is the ability to manipulate verbal and numerical symbols ... that occupies the highest position on the prestige scale, and consequently is the criterion for intelligence" (*ibid.*). Most of the widely used so-called intelligence tests are supposed to measure above all the ability to handle verbal and other symbols, cognitive skills that constitute what is referred to as scholastic aptitude. Thus, in the Western cultural context "intelligence" can operationally be defined as the ability to do well on the type of tests which have proved to predict scholastic or academic achievements fairly well.

A similar view, whereby "competence", "ability" or "talent" is conceived as being within the framework of values prevailing in a given historic and/or social context, is expressed by Hunt (1969, 1973). "With man's cultures becoming increasingly technological, the demand for strong backs and weak minds decreases radically while the demand increases for higher and higher proportions of people with high-level competence in the manipulations of symbols in problem-solving, and it becomes more and more important to determine the degree to which existing genotypic potential permits increasing competence and intellectual capacity" (Hunt, 1969, pp. 57–8). Most societies throughout the world, particularly in countries with a rapidly expanding industry, have gone through a process of equally rapid urbanization. People who from birth onward had been prepared for a more or less primitive agriculture have suddenly been thrown into a complex urban environment with quite other demands in terms of educated competence. The incompetence they thereby suffer Hunt (1969) compares to a disease.

Criticism directed against intelligence testing that has been launched from various quarters in recent years often stems from ideologies according to which the use of tests is a means whereby "the ruling class tries to replicate itself via the school system". Some who have been involved in the controversy on race and IQ go so far as to maintain that IQ testing is one of the means of oppressing the working people. In polemicizing against an article on IQ and social class by Eysenck (1973), Edmonds and Moore (1973) state: "Those who write IQ tests use their own perceptions of intelligent behavior to devise their measure. Thus, intelligence testing is a political expression of those groups in society who most successfully establish the behavior they value as measures of intelligence" (*op. cit.*, p. 12). The fact that so many low status children score very high on conventional intelligence tests is sufficient to challenge these sweeping statements as to their validity for individual differences. They can be considered seriously only with regard to group differences.

A relevant social status distinction in the emerging industrial society was the ability to operate with certain abstract symbols. Those who were masters in reading, writing and numerating came to the forefront – even in the estate society. In the industrial society they were promoted to the white-collar jobs. The more successful proceeded via institutions of higher learning to the professions. The great majority of those who succeeded in getting an adequate basic education were assigned routine white-collar jobs as clerks, etc. A certain amount of formal schooling beyond the minimum required in compulsory elementary schooling meant that the persons so equipped emerged from blue-collar to white-collar status.

But, as pointed out in the introduction, present-day society on the threshold to the post-industrial stage has "democratized" the skills which previously a minority possessed. Formal education has become prolonged and the majority of young people are staying in school for the main part of their teens. This has made the "white-collar line" disappear or at least become fairly blurred. Furthermore, modern technology, not least computer technology, has taken over most of the tasks that previously required routine writing and arithmetic skills and for which some special training was required. One only has to consider what has happened since the 1940's to the office work in banks, insurance companies, department stores, etc., in order to realize that the bulk of the work for which such routine skills were needed has been transferred to machines. We have now entered a stage where skills at a higher level, such as devising new systems solutions or new ways of programming, are much more in demand. This has contributed to moving the "meritocracy line" up to a higher level in terms of both the intellectual processes involved and the amount of formal education required.

DOES IQ MATTER?

Until recently most social scientists have been of the opinion that "talent", "intelligence", or "ability", as measured by IQ tests or by tests of scholastic aptitude which cover basic cognitive skills, accounts for a major portion of individual differences in life careers. It has been noted that a rank order of *mean* IQ's for various occupations is almost perfectly correlated with a rank order of the social prestige and earnings accruing to these occupations (Duncan, 1961).

As discussed more closely later (pp. 87 *et seq.*) in this book, this notion has in recent years been challenged by several researchers. In a way, the controversy over whether IQ makes much, little or no difference is somewhat confusing. Cohen (1972) rightly points out that if people with high IQ's did not have more influence than ordinary people, then there would not be much to argue about. It would seem to us that the confusion stems partly from the fact that IQ and scholastic attainment are rather highly correlated and that amount of formal education is correlated with adult earnings. Thus it is a short step to believing that IQ *per se* accounts for adult economic success.

With the exception of Jencks (1972) and his associates, Bowles and Gintis (1973) have launched the most systematic, and indeed most radical, attack on the notion that IQ (as conventionally assessed) plays any "causal" role in accounting for individual differences in economic success. After having presented what they regard as convincing, and perhaps definitive, evidence they ask themselves: Why, then, in spite of what they have shown, does IQ play such an important role in the social stratification system? Their overall answer to that question is given within the framework of the Marxist model of society. IQ and its meritocratic ramifications are used to justify the liberal-capitalist production system and the social relations which underpin the social stratification system itself. Their main proposition is that "the IQ ideology is a major factor in legitimating these social relations in the consciousness of the workers" (*op. cit.*, p. 74). Furthermore: "In advanced capitalist society the stratification system is based on what we term the hierarchical division of labor, characterized by power and control emanating from the top downward through a finely gradated bureaucratic order." This overall proposition can be broken down into the following subpropositions, which Bowles and Gintis set out to prove.

(1) The "IQ ideology serves to legitimate the hierarchical division of labor".

(2) It is "conducive to a general technocratic and meritocratic view of the stratification system that tends to legitimate ... means of allocating individuals to various levels of the hierarchy".

(3) The "IQ ideology operates to reconcile workers to their eventual economic positions primarily via the schooling experience, with its putative objectivity, meritocratic orientation, and technical efficiency in supplying the cognitive needs of the labor force".

(4) The "IQ ideology ... arose through the conscious policies of capitalists and their intellectual servants to perform the functions indicated above" (*op. cit.*, p. 74).

It is of course impossible to enter upon any fruitful critique of the propositions cited here without considering the social philosophy which underpins the massive challenge against the liberal and allegedly meritocratic conception. The general conception that "education cannot serve as a substitute for social reform" has been spelled out by the present author in a monograph on social background and educational career (Husén, 1972). But Bowles and Gintis analyze the role of the IQ ideology in the capitalist society on the overall assumption that cognitive skills or general ability, *as measured by scholastic aptitude tests or school attainments*, are of little or no importance for individual economic success in terms of adult earning. They even go a step further by asserting that the demand for better cognitive skills was of almost no importance in the setting up of modern formal school education. At least the first of these two propositions can be tested by confronting it with empirical evidence. In doing so we shall briefly summarize how Bowles and Gintis conceive the role of the educational system in acting as a stratifier. One might also, of course, ask whether and to what extent the legitimizing meritocratic element that serves as an "objective" stratifier and distributor of social roles is part and parcel only of the capitalist system (Lasch, 1973). The authors themselves point out that inherent needs of modern industrial organization and technological necessities have resulted in a system of social relations in the job world that is characterized by hierarchical relations and which exists as well in, for instance, the Soviet Union.

In a meritocratic society with a system whereby individuals are matched smoothly to jobs education allocates people to various levels of the job hierarchy (Bowles and Gintis, p. 75). The formal educational system fulfills three roles.

(1) It distributes rewards, such as marks, certificates etc., on the basis of "objectively measured cognitive achievement". It is therefore considered to be "fair" to the individual.

(2) It has to produce useful and marketable cognitive skills.

(3) Higher levels of schooling are expected to lead to economic success, to better paid jobs, etc.

How could it be, then, that in spite of the fact that IQ purportedly does not significantly determine economic or occupational success it nevertheless is regarded as so important, even among social scientists? The answer provided by Bowles and Gintis is that "talent" or "intelligence" is only *indirectly* linked to economic success via the school system which operates as a sorting and/or screening device. "Through competition, success, and defeat in the classroom, the individual is reconciled to his or her social position" (*op. cit.*, p. 78). The school with its bureaucratic order and its hierarchical lines of authority is ultimately a preparation for the working life such as the capitalists would have it (cf. Bowles, 1971). Thus, the social relations of the school correspond to those of the working life, i.e. are totalitarian, hierarchical and highly meritocratic.

We shall take issue with Bowles and Gintis with regard to their basic proposition, that of the "IQ ideology", the notion that certain cognitive skills or certain "merits" in the cognitive field are used by those owning the means of production as a justification of keeping the workers in order, to legitimize that some have more power or influence than others, etc. It has already been pointed out (by Bowles and Gintis as well) that the hierarchical and bureaucratic order of social relations can be established in a socialist society and is therefore not a unique feature of the capitalist system.

But the proposition that the modern educational system, along with the methods of assessing cognitive competence that go with it, is just a device to sort and screen people and to serve as a make-believe justification for allocating them to different levels of the hierarchy in working life deserves further scrutiny. Furthermore, the conception of the hierarchy in modern industrial society and the effect on this society of making higher education a mass commodity also deserves to be explored further.

The authors make reference to "a growing body of historical research" (p. 79) according to which the establishment of mass education in countries in the process of being industrialized did not emanate from any need to provide the workers with cognitive skills needed for job functioning. The main purpose was to "generate a disciplined industrial labor force" equipped with the proper amount of order, docility and obedience. This argument is then added to the contention that "cognitive attributes are not central to the determination of social stratification" (p. 84). There would thus be no significance given to the role played by increased literacy in the industrial development of Europe and the United States. Yet the attempt being made in the Third World during the last two decades to bring about literacy by universal primary schooling is part of a broader strategy of creating an infrastructure needed for modernization, including the establishment of an industry (Harbison, 1973). So far there is massive evidence that the rate of return of formal education both to the individual and to the society is far from negligible. The role played by specific cognitive skills as well as by specific items of information has so far not been very thoroughly surveyed. The present author and his associates made an attempt in the 1950's to map out, subject by subject and topic by topic, to what extent the competence attained at school was useful in certain occupational areas covering both manual and white-collar jobs (Husén and Dahllöf, 1960; Husén, 1965). True, the common denominators for these areas were not big but highly significant.

One should not leave out of the picture the fact that the techniques used to measure the characteristics which could be expected to be relevant to a particular occupation or occupational sector have been crude. The non-cognitive are even less correlated than the cognitive traits with measures of stratification in the job world, so that it is somewhat hazardous to maintain that these non-cognitive attributes are "integral to the stratification process" (p. 84). Little empirical evidence is at hand to justify such a conclusion. The notion that the role of formal schooling, which in many countries (both capitalist and socialist) has been extended to cover the age range from 6 or 7 up to 16 to 18, is for the majority of young people *mainly* to serve as a classification and certification apparatus serving the capitalist economy, and that what is learned by the students is of almost no relevance to their competence in a narrow sense as potential workers, is indeed a strange one.

The authors repeatedly talk about the "hierarchical division of labor, characterized by power and control emanating from the top downward through a finely gradated bureaucratic order" (*op. cit.,* p. 74). This system of labor organization allegedly is motivated by technological necessities and economic efficiency criteria. But it is contended that the division of labor in particular is a device whereby the individual worker becomes less influential in determining the work process and the conditions in the work milieu. It is in the interest of the capitalist power élite to preserve a system of hierarchical chains of authority, because this will preserve its power.

The idea of a hierarchy implies a pyramidal structure of the enterprise or the work organization. At the bottom of the pyramid we find the mass of workers, at the next level the supervisors, then the department or division heads, and at the top the executives. Regardless of how we label the occupational categories at the various levels, the basic idea is that a few at the top are in command of the masses at the bottom.

But what change in the status system can we envisage in a society where higher or post-secondary education becomes a mass commodity and loses its élitist character? In terms of formal qualifications the pyramid would then gradually take the shape of an egg with a small tip being replaced by a rounded-off top and a broad basis with a narrow one (Husén, 1968a). The great bulk of pupils in countries with high enrollment of teen-agers stay in school until the age of 17–18. In some countries already one fifth and in a few one fourth to one third of the relevant age groups go on to some kind of extended post-secondary education. This portion of the age group is expected to rise to one half, which Trow (1973) sets as the limit between "mass" and "universal" higher education. This, then, leaves only a minority at the bottom level. In Sweden, for instance, provisions in the new *gymnasium* have been made to accommodate some 90 per cent of the age groups 16 through 18, which means that roughly ten per cent would be in the bottom group. The "enrollment explosion" which has been taking place in many of the highly industrialized countries over the last two decades is in the process of changing radically the "qualification pyramid" available to the labor market during the decades to come. The few, highly qualified individuals at the top would be multiplied by a factor of at least five and the formal qualifications would spread downward. According to the "job competition" model advanced by Thurow (1972), this would mean that those with more formal education will take the job opportunities that previously were occupied by those with less education. But it will most likely also change the hierarchical structure of the work organization. The more education the workers have, the better they can get an overview of the production process and the more they will want to influence working conditions. The experiments with self-steering groups which have been going on in Scandinavia and the abolishment of the conveyor belt production model in the new Volvo factory in Kalmar, Sweden, are cases in point.

The change hinted at here will also affect the wage and salary structure. The demarcation line between manual and white-collar workers was for a long time weekly wages versus monthly salary. This line has in several countries been blurred by giving factory workers monthly salaries. The lengthening of mandatory schooling and introduction of universal secondary education have had similar effects. The system of mass higher education works against the principle of differential scarcity in determining salaries and wages.

The crucial question then is, assuming that those countries which are now highly industrialized are on the threshold of a post-industrial society à la Daniel Bell (1973), what role will education play in a society with extended schooling for young people and "recurrent" or "life-long" education for the majority of adults? How "meritocratic" will such a society become? It would be fruitful to confront the "learning society" characterized by strong meritocratic elements that Bell envisages with the "de-hierarchised" and "de-credentialized" society characterized by "full equalization of opportunity" (p. 93) according to Bowles and Gintis (1973). This "confrontation" will take place in Chapter 6 (pp. 95 *et seq.*).

AN ATTEMPT TO CONVERGE GENETIC AND SOCIOLOGICAL THINKING

Sociologists have in a way had "a vested interest in establishing a strong environmentalistic approach to the study of human behavior" (Eckland, 1967, p. 174). Many sociologists and cultural anthropologists have conveyed the impression that the "genetic base of man is uniform everywhere" (*ibid.*). Furthermore, it has often been assumed that the observed variations in behavior between populations, such as different ethnic groups, are solely determined by socio-cultural influences. In a presidential address to the American Sociological Association Faris (1961) stated that the limits to a nation's supply of talent was set not by genes but by environmental factors.

Another important barrier against taking genetic principles into consideration has been the values prevailing among social scientists. They have – at least until recently – been in a general way "liberal" in their social outlook and have believed in a society that is both "free" and "equal".

In an article in the *American Sociological Review*, prior to the spirited debate elicited by Jensen's *Harvard Educational Review* article in 1969, Eckland (1967) set forth a "reconsideration" of the relationship between genetics and sociology. This is an ambitious attempt to converge sociological and genetic principles with the aim of showing that together they can contribute to a better conceptualization and understanding of such processes as well as of the role of intelligence in status allocation and social mobility.

Eckland makes reference to population geneticists, such as Dobzhansky, and points out that their new approach is not to find out how much of observed variation in the phenotype is attributable to heredity and to environment respectively, but how *modifiable* the phenotypic expression of a given characteristic is by manipulation of the environment, for instance by education, and how genetic and environmental factors *interact* in creating the phenotype.

The genetic principles involved in equality of educational opportunity and its policy implications are spelled out. In the first place, in an open system that systematically strives to promote education mainly on the basis of criteria of ability, which are partly conditioned by genetic factors, one can expect a decreased within-class variance whereas the between-class variance will increase owing to accumulation of the genetic capital to upper social strata. Whether this is occurring or not can be subjected to empirical test by intergeneration-al studies, such as the one where the entire cohort of age 10 in the city of Malmö in Sweden has been followed up until the age of 45, when data were also collected about the school attainments of their children (Husén, 1969). The problem is, however, that it would be extremely difficult to draw any conclusions about genetic variability, either intra-class or inter-class, in these two generations, simply because they have been reared in two quite different types of society with vastly different provisions in terms of social welfare and education.

But even if we assume an increased social stratification on the basis of genetic factors as being an outcome of increased equality of oppor-tunity, it should be pointed out that this would still mean that great "reserves" of talent would be found in the lower classes owing to their greater absolute number (Vernon, 1963; Halsey, 1959).

Eckland also thinks that the family as an institution is highly questionable in a society that radically wants to implement a policy of equality of educational opportunity. "The task of rearing a particular child is the 'culturally-induced' responsibility of the parents who are directly related to the child but whose genetic endowments may be too poorly matched (to the child) to succeed. If our national ideals include equality of opportunity and a full utilization of all human resources and if to pursue these goals the structure of the family is so designed that children eventually must be emancipated from their families of orientation, then the obligation of parents to rear a child on account of the accident of birth is an obviously obsolete (or at least contradictory) feature of a modern society. Differential advantages and handicaps are rooted in the nature of the parent-child relation-ship" (*op. cit.*, p. 184). A genetically bright child might have dull parents who do not cater to his assets, and conversely, a genetically dull child might enjoy compensatory advantages by having genetically bright parents who will be likely to create a stimulating home for their child!

The radical, in Charles Frankel's words "redemptive", egalitarianism whose most prominent proponent is John Rawls (1971), takes the "natural lottery" of being born with a given set of genes into a given set of social conditions as a starting point for proposing a redistribution of burdens and benefits that leads to more equality. The implications with regard to the role of the family versus society at large are similar to those brought out by Eckland.

Another dilemma is the one encountered in societies with mass education at advanced levels and where education has become an important vehicle for social mobility. It is the understanding of those who favor a policy of promoting individuals who have "real talent" that insofar as selection has to take place the criteria should be based on this talent. The mere fact that enrollment has been expanded and that the system in this respect has become more open does not prevent its becoming successively more competitive in terms of pushing ahead within the system. This means not only that marking and examinations become increasingly essential features but that there is an increasing pressure for tracking, ability grouping and individualization, such as allocating slow learners to special classes, introducing enrichment programs for the gifted, etc. However, the criteria used in the selection and sorting process are not measures of "innate" or "real" ability but at best measures of phenotypic behavior.

A third dilemma is met in analyzing social mobility. Eckland points out that most studies of social mobility have been conducted on the basis of father-son comparisons under the tacit assumption that genetic ability is randomly distributed over social classes. But the correlations that exist between parents and their children are conditioned not only by the common milieu but also by common genetic factors. There is a biological tie between them. The phenotypic resemblance between children and their parents is due to both environmental and genetic factors.

In Ralph Linton's (1936) classic distinction between "ascriptive" and "achieved" status, "achievement" refers to "allocation of status on the basis of properties not assigned by birth, such as class, sex, race, but ones over which the individual presumably has some control and, therefore, 'merits'. In other words, the individual's *private* capacities are involved" (Eckland, *op. cit.*, pp. 193–4). In a way, capacities constituting such things as scholastic ability and educational motivation are no more "private" than social class, sex and ethnicity. Therefore, according to the radical view, allocation to status on the basis of "ability" can be conceived of to be "ascriptive" in the same sense as that made on the basis of social background. There is, indeed, ample justification to raise the question of the justification of equating inborn capabilities to familial social background.

Criteria of status assignment and allocation to prestige positions have become burning issues in modern industrial and post-industrial society, where educated ability or competence has become increasingly important as a determiner of social mobility. The reason why they have been dealt with in a more global way in this context is that they are closely related to attempts to conceptualize "talent" or "intelligence". We shall have to come back to these problems in Chapters 5 and 6.

CHAPTER 3

"POOL OF TALENT" – CONCEPTUALIZATION AND METHODOLOGY OF ASSESSMENT

MOTIVES FOR A BETTER UTILIZATION OF THE POOL OF TALENT

There have been several motives behind the concern about how the educational system promotes or utilizes the potential scholastic talent in a nation. The weight given to these motives has differed from country to country.

(1) Equality of educational opportunity became a policy target of high priority in several West European countries after 1945. The British Labour Party, when it took over the government in 1945, pushed for the establishment of comprehensive secondary schools which would replace the dual or tri-partite secondary school system established by the 1944 Education Act and bring children from all walks of life in a given area under one roof. This was expected to facilitate greater parity of esteem between various secondary programs and thereby enhance the chances for lower class pupils to enter academic programs. The Swedish Education Act in 1950, as well as subsequent legislation leading up to complete structural reshaping of the entire school system in the 1960's, was conceived within the framework of establishing greater equality of opportunity (Husén, 1962; Tomasson, 1965; Paulston, 1968). Surveys conducted of the participation rate at upper secondary and university level showed glaring discrepancies between various social strata (Boalt, 1947; Moberg, 1951). The proportions of upper, middle and lower class in the population in the North and West European countries in the 1940's and 1950's were roughly 10, 40 and 50 per cent respectively. During these two decades their representation among matriculants or students entering the institutions of higher learning were roughly 50–60, 40–45, 5–10 per cent. This meant, then, that those whose parents were manual workers, farmers or tenant

farmers had a chance of 1–2 percent of matriculating as compared to 50–80 per cent among those whose parents were civil servants, professionals or top managers. Even if more high-level, inherited ability were assumed to have accumulated more in the upper social strata, the distribution of intelligence and achievement test scores showed enough overlap between strata to indicate that the discrepancy went far beyond any conceivable genetic difference in the between-social-class distribution of scholastic abilities (Husén, 1946).

The great imbalance in participation between upper and lower strata as compared to the considerable overlap in tested scholastic ability or in marks obtained in the common elementary school gave rise to the concept of a "reserve of ability". The "reserve" consisted of able pupils with lower class background who did not enter the university-preparing secondary school and subsequently the university. It was felt that the reasons for this were mainly economic and geographic: lack of financial means to enter further education above the mandatory school and (particularly among children from rural areas) the lack of access to a furthergoing school in the neighborhood. The way to rectify this would be to change the structure of the school system so as to keep the pupils together as long as possible and to facilitate access by various financial means, such as the abolishment of school fees and the introduction of allowances and stipends.

The very expression "reserve of ability" (*begåvningsreserv, Begabungsreserve*) was coined by Dr. Ragnar Edenman, who at that time served as an expert in the Swedish Ministry of Education in his capacity as chairman of the Royal Commission on Student Aid. In an address to the Congress of the Confederation of Swedish Student Unions in 1948 he explicitly referred to those of lower class background who evidently had the ability but not the opportunity to benefit from higher education as the "reserve of ability". Edenman later became the first chairman of the 1955 Royal Commission on University Reform. The commission conducted another survey (Härnqvist, 1958) which marked a breakthrough in the methodology of assessing the "reserve" of ability and gave rise to a vigorous policy debate in Sweden (Husén, 1972).

(2) At the beginning of the 1960's there was a rapidly growing belief in a close connection between education and economic growth (Schultz, 1961; Becker, 1964; Harbison and Myers, 1964). In the 1950's several economists had begun to study the "rate of return" to both the indi-

vidual and the national economy of the amount of formal education that the young people had absorbed. In addition to research and development, basic and further education was considered to be a vitally important contributing factor to economic growth. In one of the background reports to the OECD Policy Conference in Washington, DC in 1961 Professor Svennilson pointed out: "Economic growth is generated not only by real capital in the forms of tools and machinery, but also by men. And just as technological improvements increase the efficiency of the machinery, so education increases the efficiency of the manpower" (OECD, 1962, p. 23). In the same document Svennilson also dealt with the pool of ability and noted: "One thing that can be said with some confidence to those who fear the effect of quantitative expansion on quality is that there is certainly a much larger 'reserve of ability' that has yet to be tapped". This, he went on to say, even applied to the United States with its high enrollment ratio as compared to that of Europe. It is even more applicable to most of the European countries, where "the reservoir of untapped talent is much larger than in the United States" (*op. cit.*, p. 34).

Since the utilization of talent was conceived of as a major factor accounting for economic growth, the establishment of greater equality of opportunity could be an important strategy in promoting such a goal. This gave an extra impetus to those who thought that education could be used as a primary change agent in society. By changing the school structure and by establishing greater formal equality, for instance by providing financial aid, one would level out the disparities between social strata in their participation in advanced education. This was the background for the Kungälv Conference in 1961 on "Ability and Educational Opportunity" (Halsey, 1961).

(3) A third motive was also forceful in eliciting governmental support for higher education and for research and development. In most European countries there was a serious shortage of highly trained manpower right from the end of the war. This shortage was particularly serious with reference to certain key professional groups regarded as essential for economic progress, such as engineers and scientists. The same problem beset the United States in spite of the tremendous increase in college and university enrollment which had already taken place in the 1940's. The four national research councils in the United States in 1949 appointed a Commission on Human Resources and Advanced Training. The Commission sponsored an extensive study on

"America's Resources of Specialized Talent" which was directed by Dael Wolfle (1954). The keynote was set by the introductory chapter "Educated Manpower: A National Resource". The first paragraph reads: "With only 6 per cent of the world's land and 7 per cent of its population, the United States publishes 27 per cent of the world's newspapers, owns 31 per cent of all radio and television sets, produces 40 per cent of all electric power, uses 58 per cent of the world's telephones, and drives 76 per cent of its automobiles" (*op. cit.*, p. 1). Reference was made to the "international tug of war: survival itself may depend upon making the most effective use of the nation's intellectual resources. The recognition that much of America's strength comes from its educational accomplishments has led other nations to attempt a similar road to national strength". Reference was further made to the Soviet Union, which had succeeded not only in launching mass education but also in increasing its number of high level scientists and engineers in some fields more rapidly than had the United States (*op. cit.*, pp. 4–5).

An extra concern was added to this when a few years later the first Sputnik was orbited. In the same year, 1957, the United States Office of Education published a study of Soviet Education that seemed to confirm the notion reflected in the quotation above, namely that the technological achievement behind the Sputnik was due to the superior "productivity" of Soviet education. This was a period of almost masochistic self-criticism in the United States, and Admiral Rickover suddenly became one of the major experts in education. Massive support for higher education was provided in 1958 by the legislation passed in the Congress under the misleading label of the National Defense Education Act.

WHAT SHOULD BE MEANT BY "POOL OF ABILITY"?

As noted above, the catchphrase "reserve of ability" was a label designed for those pupils (mostly of lower class background) who according to conventional criteria, such as IQ and marks obtained during mandatory schooling, were "academic material" but who did not have the opportunity to go on to further schooling. The metaphor "reserve" is, of course, misleading, because it implies that there is a genetically given, "innate" and limited reservoir of talent or ability that can be utilized or not. In his report from the Kungälv conference Halsey (1961) strongly underlines that terms like "reserve of ability" or "pool of ability" are misleading, because they convey a static conception of the available talent. They are also conducive to the notion that the establishment of formal opportunity in terms of access, and means to access, would suffice to bring about more equity. He points out that social stratification should be looked upon more as something affecting educability in general and less as a barrier to formal opportunity. The phrase "reserve of ability" prevents or discourages us from realizing that ability can be *generated* by a concerted social and educational policy. A similar view was expressed by Vernon (1963) in a brief to the Robbins Commission on university education. He opposed the view that there existed in the population "a fixed distribution or 'pool' of intelligence" that would limit the number of students capable of higher education or determine the standards that those who are admitted would be capable of achieving. Vernon put more stress on the attitudinal factors and the preparation that the individual received during the early stages of his education than on IQ. A more dynamic conception of ability emerged from the methodological debate on the "reserve of ability" that took place in Sweden, spurred by the surveys conducted in the 1940's (Husén, 1946, 1947, 1948; SNS, 1950) and the 1950's (Härnqvist, 1958).

Estimates of the size of the "reserve of ability" in the surveys conducted in Sweden in the 1940's (Husén, 1946) were based on the use of intelligence test scores for entire age groups of males, the 20-year-olds who were called up for conscription. Ekman (1949) pointed out that a criterion such as an intelligence test score has its limitations. At best an intelligence test correlates (after errors of measurement have been taken into consideration) .7 with the number of years of schooling. This means that only 50 per cent of the variance in formal schooling is accounted for by the measured intelligence. This imperfection of the criterion means that the overlap of "true" scholastic ability between the subgroups is larger than the observed one based on the test score. Thus, the method of overlap tends to overestimate the size of the "reserve". In order to take the imperfection of the validity of the criterion of scholastic aptitude into account one should, according to Ekman distinguish between a reserve in a wide sense and one in a narrow sense. The former includes *all* the factors determining scholastic achievement, both the cognitive and the affective, whereas the latter is limited to those cognitive abilities which are covered by the test instrument. Ekman suggests that an estimation based on what the test measures should be referred to as an "intelligence reserve".

The group intelligence test employed in assessing the "reserve of ability" in Sweden in the 1940's was the verbally-oriented classification test administered to the 20-year-old concripts when they were called up. At that age practically all differentiation with regard to formal schooling had occurred. The great majority had left school at the age of 14 or 15 at the end of seven or eight years of compulsory schooling. Less than 20 per cent had gone on to the academic lower secondary school or to some kind of vocational school. Less than 10 per cent had entered the upper secondary school (*gymnasium*) which prepared for university entrance. Less than 5 per cent had sat for the matriculation examination which qualified for university entrance.

But formal schooling as such turned out to affect the criterion, i.e., the group intelligence test score. In a ten-year follow-up it was shown that additional formal schooling leading to the matriculation examination meant a boost of about 10 IQ points (Husén, 1951b). Härnqvist (1968), who used a more sophisticated method of estimating the "boost", found that it was about one standard deviation, i.e., some 15 IQ points. In comparing 20-year-olds having only elementary school education with those who had reached the matriculation examination this systematic error of "boosting" tended to reduce the overlap of distribution of scores and thus to underestimate the size of the "reserve".

Ekman (1951) also developed a probability method, which (provided its assumptions are valid) yields much more accurate estimations of the "reserve of ability" than the overlap method. His method, which will be described later, is based on one explicit and one implicit assumption. In the first place, it assumes that practically all upper-class or upper middle-class children who have the minimum aptitude to benefit from post-compulsory academic school are given the opportunity to enter and pursue such schooling. Considering the fact that at that time (around 1950) some 80–90 per cent of children with upper or upper-middle class background went on to such education this seems to be a valid assumption. Thus, the transfer rate and completion rate at each level of ability (according to such criteria as test scores or school marks) in the top stratum could be regarded as the probability of transfer and completion under "optimal" conditions.

The probability method furthermore builds on the implicit assumption that genetically inherited ability is randomly distributed over social classes. This has since then become an emotionally loaded issue. Eckland (1967) in his review of the relationship between sociology and genetics points out that the IQ correlations between parents and their children cannot entirely be accounted for by their shared milieu. One, therefore, has to assume that social classes differ somewhat with regard to the distribution of genetic capacities for intellectual performance. But the distributions of genetic capacities are so diversified that the likelihood for large differences is indeed small (Dobzhansky, 1973).

Finally, it ought to be made quite explicit that the model assumes a utopia where *all* children share the material and cultural advantages of those who are born and reared in the upper social stratum. The implementation of a social experiment to test this assumption would, however, take several generations in view of the inertia due to the "social heredity" from one generation to the next. Thus, for example, when asked what level of education they aspired to for their own children, twice as many of upper class background hoped for university education as among those whose own parents were working class (Husén, 1968b). These differences in aspiration appeared in spite of the fact that in the intervening 30-some years education had become formally accessible to all. No fees were required and allowances and stipends for those who went on had become available.

METHODS OF ASSESSING THE POOL OF TALENT

It was mentioned earlier that Swedish surveys of the social composition of enrollment in academic secondary schools and universities had revealed striking disparities in participation between the various social strata. In the 1940's and early 1950's young people whose parents belonged to the upper or upper-middle class (professional and managerial strata) passed the matriculation examination about 20–30 times as frequently as did those with working class or farm background. (These surveys have been reviewed in Husén, 1972.) The picture was very much the same in the other West European countries. This discrepancy gave rise to the notion that there was a considerable "reserve" of untapped ability in the lower social strata. This notion was further reinforced when survey data comprising intelligence test scores for representative age samples or for entire age cohorts of pupils or adults became available, for instance as a by-product of the testing of young males called up for military service. Such survey data have been used in attempts to estimate the size of the "reserve" of ability in England (Gray and Moshinsky, 1936), the United States

(Wolfle, 1954; Flanagan *et al.*, 1964), France (Sauvy and Girard, 1965, 1970; Sauvy *et al.*, 1973), Germany (Peisert, 1967; Roth, 1971), Sweden (Husén, 1946, 1947, 1948; sns, 1950), Austria (oecd, 1965), the Netherlands (de Wolff, 1961; Spitz, 1962; Van Heek, 1968) and Denmark (Hansen, 1971;Oerum 1971). Access to intelligence and achievement test data and to school marks made it possible to measure the degree of overlap between groups with varying amounts of formal education and differing social backgrounds. These approaches to identifying the pool of ability constitute only the first steps in the development of a more sophisticated research methodology.

A brief description of the development of methods of identifying and assessing the "reserve of ability" is of interest not only from the scientific point of view. It also illustrates the interaction between research and educational policy-making, since quite a few of the Swedish investigations were initiated by Royal Commissions charged with the task of bringing about changes that were to "democratize" further education; moreover, most of the survey research before the 1960's in the field happened to be conducted in Sweden. Thus a recapitulation of the history of the surveys conducted during the two preceding decades provides a case study of the development of an important area of policy-oriented research which has had important methodological "spin-off" effects.

1) *The Actuarial Approach*

During the 1940's two Royal Commissions in Sweden dealt from different vantage points with the problem of democratizing school education. The approach used was mainly what could be labeled the actuarial or demographic, i.e., utilization of existing data. The main purpose was to provide information on how social class background was related to participation in post-compulsory (academic) education.[1]

---

[1] Since 1911 the Swedish Bureau of Census has employed a social class indexing based on parental occupational titles. These are categorized in 32 groups of which seven are referred to as upper class (Social Class 1) comprising professionals, owners of big enterprises, top managers, higher civil servants, etc. Fifteen are referred to as middle class (Social Class 2), such as farmers, salaried workers in lower positions, supervisors in industry. Finally, ten groups make up the lower class (Social Class 3) which mainly consists of wage earners and manual workers (Gesser and Fasth, 1973). As has been pointed out in another connection (Husén, 1972, p. 18 *et seq.*), the categorization into upper, middle and lower class, although it mirrors the perception of social stratification in the industrialized society, is not as clearcut as it might appear. The boundary between Social Classes 1 and 2, particularly, is somewhat blurred. It has also been pointed out that the relative status of certain groups changes, making comparisons over time

By and large, the classification into three social classes seems to be based upon a mixture of the following criteria, which are implicit as long as the only information on parental background on which the classification is based is the parents' occupational titles:

(1) Amount of *formal education*. Those who come under the upper and upper-middle class heading have university degrees that open up the road to professional occupations. Those who leave the upper stage of the elementary school after completion of the compulsory school period (which in Europe until recently has throughout meant not qualifying for white collar jobs) are heading for manual jobs. The remainder, then, with some additional formal education, comprise the middle-middle and lower-middle class which consists largely of salaried workers lacking higher education.

(2) The *status* attached to the various occupations according to a generally perceived prestige scale.

(3) *Earnings* (and wealth) implied. The owner of a big enterprise is supposed to be wealthy enough to come under the upper class bracket.

These three criteria are, of course, closely correlated with each other, particularly formal education and social status ratings. We shall not discuss here the weaknesses inherent in this classification scheme so widely used in surveys, not only in Sweden, on the pool of ability. It is enough to point out that it would be much more informative to identify certain clear-cut variables in the home background which could then be related to scholastic attainments.

The 1940 Royal Commission conducted a follow-up study of the pupils who had entered the junior secondary school (*realskola*) in 1938 and followed the cohort until 1944, when practically all pupils had either completed or dropped out from the *realskola* (sou, 1944).

The 1940 Royal Commission found that 18 per cent of the pupils who at the age of 11 entered the five-year *realskola*, which traditionally was the first step of preparation for university entrance, were of upper class origin as compared to 24 per cent coming from lower class homes. According to the election statistics, the two classes were represented

---

difficult. Thus, shop clerks have traditionally been referred to as middle class, not only because they were "white collar" workers but also because they had to possess certain competencies in coping with their role in the small shops, which many of them do not need any longer in meeting the highly specialized requirements in the supermarkets. University students have been categorized as upper class since the time when they represented far less than five per cent of the relevant age groups and when less than 10 per cent of them came from homes in the lower class bracket.

by 5 and 57 per cent among the electorate. At the age of 15–16 transfer took place to the senior secondary school (*gymnasium*), where 28 per cent of the initial enrollment came from the upper and 11 from lower class. This meant, then, that the chances for an upper class pupil to enter the *gymnasium* were about 25 times as high as for a lower class pupil (SOU, 1944). The same picture was obtained by a study which the Royal Commission on Student Aid sponsored and which reflected the enrollment pattern at the universities in the 1940's (Moberg and Quensel, 1949). The social selection process had advanced further so that among the students enrolled at the universities 58 per cent were of upper and only 6 per cent of lower class background. Moberg (1951) conducted a study of the social class background of 5 cohorts of Swedish university undergraduates, those who enrolled in 1910, 1920, 1930, 1937 and 1943 respectively. The proportions between social classes remained remarkably constant over more than 30 years:

Social Class Background	Enrollment year				
	1910	*1920*	*1930*	*1937*	*1943*
1	35	35	37	36	32
2	55	54	51	52	56
3	9	10	11	9	10
Unknown	1	1	1	3	2
Total	100	100	100	100	100

Three additional studies, based not only on actuarial data but also on tests, questionnaires, etc., should be mentioned as well because of their methodological significance and their impact on policy making. Neymark (1952) in 1948 drew a 10 per cent sample of all the 20-year-old conscripts, which was a fairly representative sample of all males born in 1928, and by mail questionnaires and interviews collected information on their educational and occupational careers until 1956. Although the major purpose was to study migration as related to background, the data can be used to throw light on certain social selection processes. Being an expert in vocational guidance Neymark designed his own schema of categorizing occupations and ended up with 21 main categories, presented in Table 1. For each of these categories he calculated the number of sons who obtained education through the *gymnasium* and passed the matriculation examination. Table 1 gives a more detailed picture of the situation in the 1940's that I have already described by means of more global figures. Some 70–80 per cent of sons of high civil servants and managers had matriculated as compared to less than five per cent among farmers and workers.

TABLE 1: *Number of Sons (in per cent) by Parental Occupational Category Going to Academic Secondary School*
(Survey based on a 10 per cent sample of all male 20-year-olds born in 1928)

	Proportion Having passed Matriculation Examination (per cent)	Proportion Having passed Middle-School Examination (per cent)
A. Farmers		
(1) Farm Owners	2	3
(2) Tenant farmers	2	2
B. Small-farm owners:		
(1) Farming, gardening, forestry, etc.	0	0
(2) Farm labourers with small-holdings	1	1
C. Fishermen	0	0
D. Small merchants	11	21
E. Small manufacturers and artisans	9	9
F. Building contractors	9	13
G. Repairmen	0	9
H. Taxi owners, etc.	2	13
I. Civil servants:		
(1) With university training	80	11.5
(2) Other specialized training	53	21.5
J. Managers	70	17
K. Middle and low grades of managerial posts	23	34.5
L. Supervisors and technicians:		
(1) In public service with assignments not requiring advanced general education	15	35
(2) Privately employed	8	20
(3) Foremen	3.5	14
M. Salesmen	2	8
N. Workers in public services:		
(1) Firemen, policemen, coastguards, etc.	2	23
(2) Transport workers, (railway, bus, tramway), postmen	5	9.5
O. Skilled workers in industry:		
(1) Construction workers	2.5	7.5
(2) Craftsmen (skilled carpenters, mechanics, etc.)	3	12
P. Semi- or unskilled construction workers:		
(1) In public services	1.5	13
(2) Road workers, railway workers	0	1.5
(3) Construction workers, (building industry)	0	3
Q. Workers in industry of other categories than O and P	1	5
R. Forestry workers	0	2
S. Farm labourers (other than B (2) above)	0.5	1
T. Workers in transport & distributive trades	0	3
U. General labourers	3	3

Source: Neymark, 1952.

Two follow-up studies limited to big cities and, as far as school education is concerned, reflecting the situation in the 1940's were conducted by Boalt (1947) and Husén (1950, 1951b). The first was based on a cohort of 4,895 pupils in the city of Stockholm who in 1936 had completed the fourth grade of the elementary school and were eligible for entrance into the academic secondary school. They were followed up through the end of the *gymnasium*, i.e., grade 13, and their educational attainments were related to social class, parental income and welfare record. A basic concept used throughout the study was that of "social handicap", which Boalt defined as the correlation between a social background variable and a criterion of educational attainment, when measures of ability, such as test scores or school marks, had been partialed out. The partial correlations between attainment variables on the one hand and social class and parental income on the other are given in Table 2. Social class evidently exerts a strong "threshold effect" when it comes to transfer from one level to another in the hierarchy of formal education, something that can be expected considering the large disparities in participation between the social classes. The other attainment variables are only slightly affected by social

TABLE 2: *Social Handicap in Selection for and in Screening within the Academic Secondary School. (Handicap defined as partial correlation of selection or screening with social factor)*

Stage:	Parental Socio-economic Status	Parental Income
Selection/non-selection for realskola (second. acad. school) at 11	0.57	0.25
Screening in realskola	0.17	0.28
Selection/non-selection for gymnasium at 15–16	0.47	0.45
Screening in gymnasium	0.15	0.07

Source: Boalt, 1947.

handicap. It should, however, be kept in mind that by partialing out ability one also partials out the variance common to social class and test scores or social class and school marks.

The other survey consisted of all third-graders (about 1,500) in the city of Malmö in 1938. The majority of these pupils were born in 1928. The males were called up for conscription in 1948 (Husén, 1950). The subjects were contacted in 1963 and information about their careers since the beginning of the 1940's was collected by mail questionnaires and interviews. Thus, social background, intelligence test scores and school marks in 1938 could be related to their subsequent educational and occupational careers (Husén, 1969). The subjects were contacted again in 1972, and the actuarial data on the school attainments of their children were collected as well as data about the subjects themselves from the Social Welfare and Criminal Register. As far as transfer to non-compulsory, mostly academic secondary education is concerned we found large differences between the four strata (the lower class having been split into skilled and unskilled manual occupations). Whereas 85 per cent of those with upper or upper-middle class background had obtained some kind of academic secondary education (even if it lasted only a few years), the corresponding figure of the lower-lower class was only 12 per cent (Husén, 1950). It is important to note that the secondary education schools were within close geographic reach of all strata since the students all lived in the same city.

2) The "Cutting-Score" or "Overlap" Approach

Swedish legislation on conscription provided that all 20-year-old males have to appear before a Conscription Board where they go through a psychological and medical examination. Thus intelligence test scores, data on educational attainments and vocational experiences are available for almost complete age cohorts, affording a unique opportunity to study the relationship between educational attainments and ability according to the classification test in representative groups.

The first in a series of such surveys was conducted in 1945 (Husén, 1946) comprising more than 44,000 conscripts born in 1925 and consisting of about 95 per cent of the relevant age group. Distributions on the intelligence test were obtained for the various levels of formal schooling: elementary school only (which was the compulsory 6–8 year school); middle school (*realskola*) without leaving certificate; *realskola* with leaving certificate; *gymnasium* without matriculation examination; *gymnasium* with matriculation examination; and university studies. The potential academic school population or "reserve of ability" was then determined on the basis of an analysis of the overlap between the distributions and under certain assumptions. The assumptions were in the first place that the test was a satisfactorily valid measure of scholastic ability and that formal schooling did not considerably affect the "true" scores of the various subgroups. As has been spelled out above (p. 42), neither of these assumptions was strictly valid. Test scores on the average account for only about 50 per cent of the variance in scholastic attainment and the full academic secondary school (social background being kept under control) adds some 10 to 15 IQ points to IQ as measured by conventional tests.

The assessment of the potential middle school (*realskola*) population was carried out according to the following procedure. The distribution for those who had completed the *realskola* was compared with that for those who, mostly because of failure to meet academic standards, had dropped out during the four- or five-year course. The latter group made up about 50 per cent of the entering cohort. An additional 10–15 per cent repeated one or more grades before they obtained the certificate. The average number of pupils not being promoted at the end of each school year was about 10 per cent. Based on the number of those completing the course in spite of their not being considered intellectually qualified for the academic secondary school, a cutting score was set at the tenth percentile (equal to IQ = 107) for that particular group. This, somewhat arbitrary, score happened to cut the distribution of those who dropped out from the *realskola* at about the median. Several educators having experience with the academic secondary school were of the opinion that roughly half of those who failed the *realskola* did so mainly because of intellectual shortcomings. This observation, for what it is worth, was used as an additional rationale for arbitrarily setting the cutting score for "*realskola* capability" at the tenth percentile in the test distribution of the *realskola* graduates.

It was found that 33 per cent of the entire age group scored on the IQ scale 107 or above. The corresponding figure for the elementary school distribution was 20 per cent. Since those who had finished their formal schooling with only elementary school consisted of about 80–85 per cent of the age group, it was evident that the potential *realskola* "reserve" was enormous. Only some 15 per cent entered the junior secondary school and about half of these graduated and/or proceeded to the senior secondary school.

When the same technique was applied in comparing those who entered the upper secondary school (*gymnasium*) and dropped out with those who completed their pre-university studies by passing the matriculation examination, it was estimated that about 12 to 14 per cent of

the entire age group had the intellectual capability to pass the matriculation examination, i.e., could qualify for university entrance.

The same model of assessment was employed in four subsequent
surveys conducted on the age groups called up for conscription in 1945,
1946, 1947 and 1948 (Husén, 1946, 1947, 1948; SNS, 1950). The group
test used in 1946 and 1947 was very much the same as in 1945, whereas
a complete new test was devised for 1948 (Husén and Henricson, 1951).
This new test was then partially revised for the next cohort tested in
1949 (SNS, 1950). The estimations arrived at from the age groups 1945
through 1949 have been collated in Table 3.

TABLE 3: *Estimates (in per cent) of the number of Individuals within Total
Age Groups capable of passing Lower Secondary School Examination and
University Entrance Examination (Studentexamen)*

Age Group	Proportion of Individuals above Cutting Score for Lower Secondary School Examination		Proportion of Individuals above Cutting Score for University Entrance Examination	
	Within Total Age Group (per cent)	Among Those with Elementary Schooling only (per cent)	Within Total Age Group (per cent)	Among Those with Elementary Schooling only (per cent)
1945	33	22	14	5
1946	32	20	13	5
1947	32	19	12	4
1948	33	22	13	5

Sources: Husén, 1946; Husén, 1947; Husén, 1948; SNS, 1950.

The surveys and follow-up studies conducted by Husén (1946, 1947
and 1948) and Boalt (1947) were quoted in the Education Bill on the
comprehensive school submitted to the 1950 session of the Swedish
Parliament. The Bill drew the conclusion that particularly in the lower
class there obviously existed a vast untapped "reserve of talent". It
recommended that as an act of justice it should be seen to that children
of underprivileged background were given the opportunity to gain admission to further education inasmuch as they might well be able to
benefit from it.

The estimates of the size of the "reserve" triggered a debate among
both educators and social scientists in the late 1940's and early 1950's.
The notion that enrollment in academic secondary schools could be
expanded several times without lowering intellectual standards for

admission did not seem plausible. Similar arguments had been advanced in the United States during the 1920's and 1930's when high school enrollment increased heavily (Finch, 1946). Quensel (1949), a statistician, criticized the surveys mainly on account of the error of measurement but overlooked the much more important source of error which stemmed from the lack of validity of the test instrument (Ekman, 1949). The established fact that only 1–2 per cent of the children of working class background progressed so far in the academic secondary schools as to become eligible for university entrance did not seem to constitute any source of concern or raise any questions about equality of opportunity. Quensel warns his readers against the belief that there could be any considerable reservoir of talent.

3) *The Probability Approach*

As mentioned earlier, a breakthrough in conceptualization and sequential to that in the methodology applied in assessing the size of the "reserve of talent" was achieved in two articles by Ekman (1949, 1951). A distinction between "reserve" in a wider and in a narrow sense was based on the fact that the measuring instrument included only intellectual and non-cognitive factors. Ekman made a further distinction between a *potential* "reserve" and a realized or *actual* "reserve". This distinction took into account that the test data could have been collected after the differentiation of formal schooling had occurred, which meant that the IQ's for those with several years of academic schooling above the mandatory school leaving age were "boosted" between one half to one standard deviation. Tests administered at the age of 20 therefore gave "unduly" high scores to those who had spent the years from ages 14 to 20 in school, whereas those who had had little experience in verbal activities were at a disadvantage. This fact, of course, tended to underestimate the size of the pool of talent.

The method employed in the probability approach is, as was mentioned above, based on the assumption that all upper class children who have the potential are given the opportunity to enter institutions of further education. The method also makes an implicit assumption which is not even hinted at, namely, that genetic ability is randomly distributed in all social strata. Halsey (1959) made this assumption explicit in debating with Burt about innate differences between social classes.

According to this approach, the number of upper class pupils at each level of the criterion (score bracket or mark) who reach a given level in the hierarchy of formal education serves as a measure of the probability of what will happen if a child at a given level is given upper class opportunities. Thus, by multiplying the number of children at each ability level with the respective probability values one arrives at an estimate of how many in each stratum are likely to be able to advance in the system to a certain level. The probabilities for transfer from one level to another and for completing the course at each level are exclusively derived from Social Class 1.

With such a methodology one arrives, in Ekman's terminology, at a "potential reserve in the wider sense", that is, what is predicted to happen if children from the other social strata are given the same overall opportunities as those from the upper class.

Developing further the ideas proposed by Ekman (1951), Härnqvist (1958) carried out an investigation, sponsored by the 1955 University Commission, which has so far been the most important contribution to the research in this field. Härnqvist adopted and developed further the probability method suggested by Ekman. Later de Wolff applied the same idea in conducting a study based on data on Dutch servicemen. Both Härnqvist's and de Wolff's methodological considerations are presented in the report from the Kungälv conference sponsored by OECD on "Ability and Educational Opportunity" (Halsey, 1961).

The assumption of random distribution of inherited ability among social classes not only is open to question, but as a basis for policy recommendations envisions a Utopia difficult to realize.

Härnqvist arrived at the estimate that close to 28 per cent of an age cohort at that time was able to reach and pass the matriculation examination, i.e., qualify for university entrance. In that particular year (1956) 8.2 per cent actually passed the examination. Another 4.1 per cent of the age cohort in the "reserve" were pupils who had obtained the junior secondary school certificate but had not gone on to the senior secondary school. The majority of the "reserve", however, consisted of 15.5 per cent of the age group who had left school after completion of mandatory elementary schooling. Subsequent expansion of upper secondary education in Sweden came close to Härnqvist's estimates from the first half of the 1950's. When the matriculation examination was abolished in 1968, the proportion of an age group having attained that level in the system was about 22 per cent. The 1964 Education Act made provisions for 30 per cent of an age cohort to enter the university-preparing *gymnasium*.

THE EFFECT OF FORMAL SCHOOLING UPON IQ

We have noted earlier that most of the debate on the proper utilization of talent which took place in the 1950's and early 1960's was based on two by and large tacit assumptions.

(1) Intelligence or talent as both an individual and a national asset is something *fixed*. It is in the interest of the individual that his innate capacity be optimally developed, because his personal career and well-being depends on it. As far as the nation is concerned, there is a given capital of inherited intelligence unequally distributed among the individuals, and the economic and competitive power of the nation is dependent upon the efficient utilization of this talent, particularly of the specialized kind that can be employed in science and technology.

(2) The development of intelligence is largely *predetermined*. Learning in general and formal schooling in particular have to operate within a rather narrow "margin" of inherited capabilities which unfold according to a predetermined pattern.

These assumptions have repeatedly been challenged by research conducted during the last 10–15 years, not least that which has been done in the field of pre-school education (Hunt, 1973). Longitudinal studies have enabled us to study the long-range effect ("social inheritance") of certain environmental influences. It would take us too far afield to try to review here the research that has challenged the notions of fixed intelligence and predetermined development. Since the present author has had the opportunity to follow over a long period the cognitive development of a large group of young people and to relate their intellectual performance to the amount of formal schooling they had obtained, we shall limit ourselves here to the problem of whether and to what extent the "IQ capital" can be increased by the learning experiences obtained in the ordinary school. If IQ as defined by conventional, verbally-oriented intelligence tests is a valid measure of scholastic ability – and it is by definition, since the tests have as a rule been validated against operational criteria of school attainments – and if it can be systematically affected by formal schooling, then one can increase the intellectual capital to the extent that one can "improve" intelligence. Acceptance of this point of view would have important repercussions on the conception of how the "pool of talent" should be taken care of. Instead of a strategy of scarcity, whereby a high proportion of the educational resources would have to be allocated to those pupils or groups of pupils who are diagnosed as belonging to the élite, a more generous strategy of equality could be employed that would benefit pupils at all levels of ability.

Some 700 individuals who were tested in the third grade in 1938 at the modal age of 10 were retested in 1948 with a group intelligence test when they were registered for conscription (Husén, 1950, 1951b and 1969). This made it possible to assess the systematic effect on IQ of formal schooling after the age of 10. In 1938 all had the same amount of schooling, whereas in 1948 at the age of 20 the whole range of differentiation from seven years of compulsory elementary schooling up to some university education was represented. The IQ difference between the 1938 and the 1948 scores for each individual was calculated and after due consideration had been given to the so-called regression effect caused by lack of reliability of the test, adjusted differentials could be calculated for each level of formal schooling.

The mean difference in IQ between 1938 and 1948 for those who had continued in lower and upper secondary academic school and thereby qualified for university entrance was a gain of 11 IQ points, whereas those who had left school after completing the seven compulsory years lost one point. (Husén, 1951b). Using the same data Härnqvist (1959), with another technique for estimating the effect of further schooling, has found the difference between the two groups to be even larger, setting it at about one standard deviation, i.e., about 15 IQ points.

Two additional observations are of some import. The same amount of further formal schooling tended to increase the intellectual performance, more in pupils from upper social strata than in pupils from lower strata. That is, those whose parents represented the professional, semi-professional and managerial status tended to further outdistance the others (skilled and unskilled workers) during the ten-year period. Whereas the portion of the total variance in IQ due to the spread *between* the different levels of schooling had increased during the ten-year period, it had decreased *within* these levels which have thus become more homogeneous. The variance between levels of schooling in per cent of the total variance increased from 20 in 1938 to 39 in 1948; whereas the variance within the levels decreased from 80 to 61 per cent (Husén, 1950, p. 114 *et seq.*).

CONCLUDING REMARKS

Survey research on the availability of talent and the closely related problem of the "reserve of ability" was launched in the 1940's. At the outset it was inspired by policies in Western Europe and the United States of equalizing access to education beyond mandatory schooling. Later, when demands for highly trained manpower as well as social demands for further education grew rapidly, education began to be regarded not only as "consumption" but also as a major force in economic growth. A third motive behind national efforts to assess the extent to which existing talent was properly utilized was the growing realization that skilled manpower had a key role to play in international competition, particularly in an age when international trade was rapidly expanding and regional common markets, trade as well as labor markets, began to emerge.

The concept of the "pool of ability", as well as the "reserve of ability", were at the outset shaped within the framework of a static, hereditarian view of availability of talent. Each individual was born with a by and large fixed amount of ability (mostly identified as a scholastic ability). Steps should be taken on the part of society, as a rule by certain policies implemented by the state, to remove the economic and geographical barriers preventing the talented individual from getting access to the high level of education that his endowment entitled him to. Once having been granted access it was up to the individual to take optimum advantage. Talent was limited and in short supply, and it would be to the benefit of both the individual and society at large if it were properly utilized.

The methodology of assessing the "reserve of talent", i.e., the proportion of the relevant age group that was likely to profit from education at the secondary and tertiary levels, grew more sophisticated as the conceptualization became more accurate and the survey techniques more adequate. At the beginning rather simple demographic or actuarial methods were employed in determining the participation rates in higher education among various socio-economic groups. Large-scale testing programs, such as those in elementary schools or at induction to military service, provided an opportunity to relate ability (as measured by the standardized tests) to social background and scholastic attainments. Thereby crude estimations of the "reserve" could be arrived at. The so-called probability method represented a big step forward in sophistication and was able to provide more accurate estimations.

In the wake of the survey research, as well as studies of a more experimental or interventionist character, there has been a growing realization that at the phenotypic level neither individual ability nor the "pool" or "reserve" constituted by a group of individuals can be regarded as a strictly limited or fixed capital; they are, rather, assets that can be affected by changes that take place in the society in which the individual grows up. Thus, for instance, additional schooling at the secondary and tertiary levels could "boost" the IQ as measured by conventional intelligence tests considerably. Expanded schooling and improved social conditions most likely account for the major portion of the rising average IQ.

CHAPTER 4

THE SECULAR TREND IN THE DEVELOPMENT
OF THE POOL OF ABILITY

THE ISSUE AND ITS BACKGROUND

It was pointed out earlier that rather early in the intelligence test movement it became almost an axiom that test scores reflected a fixed capacity which was set in an individual by his genes (Cronbach, 1973). Hunt (1969) points out, however, that the father of the first viable method of measuring intelligence, Alfred Binet, strongly protested against the "brutal pessimism" that intelligence was a fixed quantity. He compared a child's mind to the barren land from which the farmer by means of improved methods of cultivation could take good harvests. When, in the wake of Army Alpha, group intelligence tests began to be employed on a large scale in the schools and survey data became available, test scores were related to various background variables. One of these was size of family. Sutherland and Thomson (1926) presented evidence from surveys conducted in England that test scores were negatively correlated with family size; that is, children from families with many children scored on the average lower than those from families with only one or two children. This, of course, gave rise to concern not only among geneticists with an inclination toward eugenics but also among psychologists who in the tradition of Galton, Stanley Hall, Goddard and Terman believed in heredity as a determiner of intelligence and a pre-determiner of development.

J. McVicker Hunt (1961, 1969) has pointed out that the eugenics movement, which originated in England, had a strong impact on the intelligence test movement in the United States. Francis Galton and, of course, Charles Darwin strongly influenced the *Altmeister* of American psychology, G. Stanley Hall, who in his autobiography refers to Darwinism as "music to my ears" and several of whose students were instrumental in launching the intelligence test movement in the United States. These included Henry Goddard, F. Kuhlmann and

Lewis Terman (Cronbach, 1973). All held the view that by and large the development of intelligence was determined by heredity. Intelligence tests were supposed to spearhead social improvement by promoting the highly able and to give the rational basis for proper eugenic action with regard to the backward or retarded. Terman (1919) made a strong plea that teachers learn to use intelligence tests. In his book on the intelligence of school children he emphasizes: "Unless the rank and file of teachers learn to use tests the universal grading of children according to mental ability must remain a Utopian dream" (*op. cit.*, p. 291).

What was referred to as differential fertility could, where it operated over several generations, be anticipated to reduce considerably the intellectual capital available. The consequences of this theory were described in a book by the British psychologist Raymond B. Cattell (1937), with the dramatic title *The Fight for Our National Intelligence*, wherein he envisaged a "galloping plunge toward intellectual bankruptcy". Cyril Burt, the hierophant of the hereditarian approach to the study of intellectual development in England, dealt with the problem of intelligence and fertility in a pamphlet (Burt, 1946) published shortly after the war. In a 1949 statement he said: "In a little over fifty years the number of pupils of 'scholarship' ability would be approximately halved and the number of feeble-minded almost doubled" (Quoted after Cook, 1951, p. 6). But at the end of the 1940's cross-sectional survey data became available for representative groups from the same populations tested many years apart. The most important of these were the surveys conducted in Scotland by Godfrey Thomson and his associates (Scottish Council, 1933, 1949, 1953; cf. Maxwell, 1961). In 1933 a group intelligence test had been administered to all the 11-year-old children who could be reached. They constituted 87 per cent of the entire age group. The survey was repeated with the same group test in 1947, when data were available for 88 per cent of the age group. Over the intervening fifteen-year period an increase of more than 2 IQ points was obtained. Cattell (1950), who in 1936 had tested and collected background information about all the 10-year-olds in Leicester, England, and who had issued the strong warning signals of a declining national intelligence level, repeated his survey in 1949 and found a significant increase of about 1.3 IQ points. The first large-scale administration of group intelligence tests had taken place during World War I when the Army Alpha and Army Beta tests were given to close to 2 million drafted men. Tuddenham (1948) in 1943 gave the Army Alpha to a representative sample of World War II conscripts and found that the median of the second sample fell at the 82nd percentile of the first distribution, which suggested a considerable increase during the 25 years that had elapsed.

To be sure, none of these findings supported the contention that the intellectual resources were waning. The paradox faced by those, such as Thomson and Burt, who had been drawing gloomy conclusions from correlations obtained between family size and measures of intelligence in the children was resolved by advancing two explanations. These were discussed at the International Congress of Psychology in Stockholm in 1951 at a session in which this author participated (Katz, 1952). Both explanations were based on the tacit assumption that the test scores mainly reflected genetic differences among the pupils. The first explanation, which seems to have some face value, was that test-taking sophistication had progressively increased and therefore could account for the change in the unexpected direction. This hypothesis was tested by Thomson and his co-workers but could not be consistently supported. The second explanation was that improvement in education in the meantime, in addition to test sophistication, was "masking" the "true" changes in intelligence. This argument was weakened by the fact that standing height behaved exactly like IQ, that is, it increased. Maxwell pointed this out at the Stockholm Congress and later documented his findings in his monograph on the Scottish Mental Survey (Scottish Council, 1953; Maxwell, 1961). He found that height in children was correlated with family size to about the same extent as was IQ. But instead of declining, the mean standing height increased from 1932 to 1947. As Anastasi (1956) points out, it is evidently pointless to say that the "true, innate" height of the persons has not increased (apart from the possibility that genes determining height might have become less frequent). *Ceteris paribus*, the same applies to the increase of mean intelligence test scores.

The next stage of debate began with the preparations for the World Population Conference in Rome in 1954 under the United Nations' auspices. UNESCO's Department of Applied Social Science convened a group of experts in early 1954 to draw up a statement which was subsequently submitted to the Rome conference. The main points made in the statement are quoted in the concluding part of this chapter (p. 80).

Following Anastasi's review (1956) in the mid-fifties of the research on intelligence and family size and its implications for the development of the intellectual potentials in national populations, rather little was done to elucidate specifically the problem of "trend of national intelligence". But the matter has recently been brought up again in the wider context of the heredity-environment controversy stirred up by Jensen's (1969) article on racial and social class differences in the *Harvard Educational Review*. Jensen's main thesis is that Whites are on the average genetically superior to Blacks with respect to higher mental processes of the type measured by IQ tests. Since the fertility rate is higher among Blacks, particularly among those of low socio-economic status, than Whites in the United States, the implication of his thesis is that the US national trend of intelligence is heading downward. Others, such as Shockley (1972a, 1972b), have been quite explicit about the eugenic steps that have to be taken in order to stop the "dysgenic" trend.

BRITISH INVESTIGATIONS OF "THE TREND OF THE NATIONAL INTELLIGENCE"

Without going into great detail, it would seem fruitful to put into perspective the debate that took place in Britain during the late 1940's and the 1950's on differential fertility and its alleged effects on the national intellectual resources. Most of the survey data – and thereby the fuel for the debate – were brought together under the auspices of the Eugenics Society over which the name of Francis Galton, Charles Darwin's cousin, loomed large. Eugenics as an academic discipline was introduced at the University of London, and the Galton Laboratory was located there. Eugenics was defined by the academics as the "study of those agencies under social control that may improve or repair the racial qualities of future generations, either physically or mentally" (quoted from Penrose, 1949, p. 17). Karl Pearson, who took over the Laboratory after Galton, pursued in his tradition further studies of "intelligence as a graded character".

The proponents of active eugenics in countries on both sides of the Atlantic had after 1920 become increasingly concerned about the fate of the human race in their countries. In Europe the data accumulated by demographers seemed to indicate that a differential birthrate caused a deterioration of the gene pool, since upper social strata and highly educated people had a lower reproduction rate than the lower class and uneducated. In the United States, Brigham, by reworking the Army data, showed that there were large ethnic and race differences that applied not only to Blacks and Whites (which was taken as self-evident) but also to various European populations of immigrants (Cronbach, 1973). Thus, West and North Europeans were supposed to be more able than East and South Europeans. Such studies had a strong policy impact and influenced the immigration policy, since they fitted prevailing stereotypes.

When World War II broke out the 7th International Congress of Genetics was in session at Edinburgh and the Congress made a statement in which classical Darwinism looms large: "The intrinsic (genetic) characteristics of any generation can be better than those of the preceding generation only as a result of some kind of *selection*, i.e., by those persons of the preceding generation who had a better genetic equipment having produced more offspring..." Since the principle of selection in modern society has been restrained by "modern civilized conditions ... some kind of conscious guidance of selection is called for" (Cook, 1951, p. 9). The quotation is taken from the book *Human Fertility* by Robert C. Cook, for many years editor of the *Journal of Heredity* and, at the time of the publication of his book, Director of the American Eugenics Society. The problem referred to was taken up under a chapter headed "The Crisis".

In 1944 the British Government appointed a Royal Commission on Population under the chairmanship of Lord Simon. The Commission presented its final report to the Government in 1949. The Eugenics Society had over the intervening years submitted quite a lot of evidence to the Commission. Godfrey Thomson, for instance, had delivered the Galton Lecture in 1945 on "The Trend of National Intelligence" (Thomson, 1946). In 1946 Cyril Burt published a pamphlet on "Intelligence and Fertility", which gave rise to a lively discussion that went on in the press and in the scholarly journals of various disciplines.

Burt's 1946 pamphlet on intelligence was subjected to critical scrutiny by Blackburn (1947), whose main argument was that the data Burt had used were intelligence test *scores* whereas the prediction of the future trend of intelligence development has to be based on *innate* intelligence. Thus, the crucial questions were to what extent do the tests measure innate intelligence, and even more important, do they measure this entity with varying degrees of imperfection on different social strata? Blackburn also pointed out that much more needed to be known about the hereditary mechanisms of intelligence before the development of any future trend could be predicted. Is, for instance, the intelligence level of an individual closer to that of his sibs than to that of his parents and his children? The criticism was, however, mainly focused on the issue of environmental influences on test scores.

Two major surveys in England in the 1930's to which Blackburn made reference, one by J. A. Fraser Roberts *et al.* (1938) and one by Moshinsky (1939), had suggested that intelligence test scores are to a varying extent influenced by social class factors. Moshinsky tested about 10,000 students and divided them according to type of school. Those who were secondary fee-payers, private school and preparatory school attenders, who by and large came from the upper social strata, showed no significant correlation between family size and test scores, whereas the group in the elementary senior classes that was left after the socially and intellectually selective schools had taken their share came up with a correlation of −.23. The lack of correlation in the first group of pupils might to some extent, as Burt (1947) pointed out in his rejoinder, be an artifact of the restriction of range in the test variable. But the negative correlation in the second group supports the hypothesis of environmental influences acting upon the intelligence level. Fraser Roberts (1938) obtained similar results from a survey on all the 9–11 year old children in the city of Bath. It should be mentioned in this connection that the first major survey in which family size and an ability measure were correlated was that by Sutherland and Thomson in the 1920's (1926). Among about 60,000 elementary school children between the ages of 11 and 13 whom they investigated there was a subgroup of some 3,100 children whose fathers were coalmine workers. The correlation between family size and test scores was −.13 for both the entire population and the subpopulation. Since the entire population was on the poor side a negative correlation of this size is consistent with an environmental interpretation of the association between the two variables.

With reference to the attempt by Barbara Burks (1928) to separate the influences of environment from hereditary background Blackburn points out: "We need to know, not the average effect of environment and heredity on test scores, but how the relative proportions of these factors differ in different environments of every kind" (*op. cit.*, p. 175). This is to say, heredity should not be conceived of as a static entity but, in Dobzhansky's (1973) words, as a process.

The first attempt to test a model of heredity-environment interaction, wherein the genetic endowment is conceived of as a stage-setter for the facilitating and inhibiting operations of environmental factors, was to be made many years later by Scarr-Salapatek (1971), whose study was dealt with in Chapter 3.

As pointed out above, the Eugenics Society in Britain was very active both in sponsoring the survey research that was conducted in England and Scotland and as a forum for the debate on eugenic problems which emerged from the contact between biological sciences, such as genetics and physical anthropology, and social sciences, such as psychology and demography. When the Government in 1944 appointed the Royal Commission on Population, the Eugenics Society at the beginning of 1945 submitted a memorandum to the Commission and later in the year presented oral evidence on the basis of that memorandum. After the Commission had presented its report in 1949, a special issue October, 1949, of the *Eugenics Review* was devoted to a review of the report with contributions by representatives of relevant disciplines. The official overall review by and large expressed satisfaction with the report, which to a great extent built on the evidence that the Society had submitted.

In the meantime the outcomes of the Scottish Mental Survey of 1947, which had partly been sponsored by the Society, had become available in preliminary publication. Godfrey Thomson had outlined some general findings in an article in the London *Times* on November 17, 1948. The final report (Scottish Council, 1949) came out in August, 1949, under the editorship of Godfrey Thomson with the title, "The Trend of Scottish Intelligence". On October 25 of the same year Thomson read a paper before the Eugenics Society on "Intelligence and Fertility", which was published the following year in the Society's journal (Thomson, 1950).

Taking note of the forecast based on surveys conducted in the 1930's that the national intelligence would decline and that this had not come true, the Royal Commission says in Chapter 15 titled "Differential Fertility":

"Bad nurture and inadequate education may mask innate intelligence or prevent its full development, but heredity puts a definite limit to what can be achieved in intelligence even with the best nurture, education and good fortune ... (The Commission, however), sees no reason to doubt that in general intelligent persons in all social groups limit the size of their families more than unintelligent" (*op. cit.*, p. 124).

The standpoint reflected in the quoted statement by the Commission was modeled after Thomson's interpretation of the findings in the

Scottish 1947 survey. In his paper read to the Society, Thomson (1950) referred to the mean score increase from 1932 to 1947 as an "apparent paradox". A general improvement in welfare during the intervening 15 years was advanced as one explanation for the increase. In a letter to the Editor of the *Eugenics Review* (April 1949, p. 56) an educational psychologist pointed out the strange logic of the hereditarians, who had suggested the operation of *environmental* influences on test scores which were used to forecast a *genetic* change in intelligence. Such a question could be raised during an era when many still asked the question "What?" instead of "How much?". Even with a heritability of 0.80 there is a considerable room for environmental influences on IQ (Bereiter, 1970).

After having dealt with what falls under the heading "influence of environment", Thomson went on to "test sophistication":

There remains in the mind, however, an uneasy fear that

"environmental improvement may be only *masking* (italics mine) a hidden selection going on behind, a steady selection which might in the long run defeat any temporary environmental improvement. Especially is this fear increased by the possibility that children of 1947, though perhaps *less intelligent in reality* (italics mine), were more accustomed to tests and were thus able to make a better score" (*op. cit.*, p. 164).

The evidence for this last hypothesis was somewhat conflicting. In those regions in Scotland where children during the intervening 15 years had been confronted more frequently with testing, the mean increase was somewhat larger than in other regions; this, however, was not the case in an English survey.

Thomson made reference to a model advanced by Penrose which assumed a very low birthrate among very retarded parents and which then could account for the "paradox" of increasing intelligence in spite of negative correlation between family size and IQ. (In 1949 there were no statistics which indicated to what extent there were adults without children on various intelligence levels.) According to Penrose's model rising intelligence and negative correlation between *family size* and intelligence were compatible. Penrose (1949), who at that time was in charge of the Galton Laboratory and in a way was the curator of the Galton legacy, read a paper before the Eugenics Society in January 1949 (before the Royal Commission had published its report). He found it appropriate to issue the following cautionary words about eugenics which, he pointed out, was beset with an "immense complexity":

"The results of experimental animal genetics must be fully appreciated, yet great caution is required in their application to human problems. The human race resembles a wild population and is not a herd of domestic and laboratory animals. It has often astonished me that advocates of race improvement are so often unaware of the difficulties in the tasks which they set themselves. Eighty years ago it seemed reasonable to Galton, on the analogy with the breeding of dogs and horses, to expect to be able to produce a superior race of men in a few generations. But knowledge of medicine and genetics has increased enormously since that time, and with it has grown the perception of our ignorance ... To lay down any rules for improvement of the human stock in the light of modern knowledge ... is pretentious and absurd. It is my personal opinion after much active research work, that active eugenical propaganda is, on the whole, inimical to the advance of scientific knowledge" (Penrose, 1949, pp. 21–22).

This statement by Penrose should be seen in its temporal context. The Royal Commission on Population was about to submit its report. On the basis of survey data on the relationship between family size and intelligence test scores, members of the Eugenic Society were strongly advocating *active* eugenic steps, such as sterilization of the mentally retarded. The Commission limited itself to recommending a "voluntary system of eugenics".

It is interesting to note that, in the wake of the issue on race and social class differences raised by Jensen's *Harvard Educational Review* article in 1969, the question of the applicability of eugenic measures has been brought up again. In a book *Genetics and Education*, where he has reprinted his articles, including the 1969 one, Jensen (1972) makes reference to problems connected with the occurrence of psychological handicaps in urban slums:

"More important than the issue of racial differences *per se* is the probability of dysgenic trends in our urban slums. The social-class differential in birth-rate appears to be much greater in the Negro than in the white population. That is, the educationally and occupationally least able among Negroes have a higher reproductive rate than their white counterparts, and the most able segment, the middle class, of the Negro population have a lower reproduction rate than their white counterparts. If social-class intelligence differences within the Negro population have a genetic component, as in the white population, this condition could both create and widen genetic intelligence differences between Negroes and whites. The social and educational implications of this trend, if it exists and persists, are enormous" (Jensen, 1972, p. 331).

On the basis of views such as these William Shockley (1972a, 1972b) a physicist at Stanford, has been suggesting voluntary sterilization.

Before looking at the salient methodological problems of research on the secular trend in the development of intellectual performances and reporting on recent studies which seem to have definitively resolved the "paradox" that emerged from the British surveys in the 1930's and 1940's, let us review the major surveys conducted both in Britain and elsewhere.

THE LEICESTER SURVEYS, 1936 AND 1949

With support by the Eugenics Society in England, Raymond B. Cattell (1937) in 1936 launched a survey with two samples: all the 10-year-olds in the city of Leicester and in a remote area of Devonshire, respectively. The findings were reported in a monograph with the dramatic title "The Fight for Our National Intelligence". The background of the study was the concern that had arisen through earlier investigations in regard to "dysgenic trends" in the development of the intelligence level. In the introduction to a later survey he stated " ... our culture is one in which greater intelligence of the population is a boon to all and in which deteriorations of the distribution can lead to misery or catastrophe ..." (Cattell, 1950, p. 136).

The 1936 survey showed that family size was negatively related to intelligence, more so in the rural than in the urban sample. On the basis of the reproduction rate as related to various levels of IQ in the *children*, Cattell arrived at the prediction that the average level of intelligence in the population at large would decrease by about one IQ point for every decade. Thus, the average decrease from 1936 to 1949 would be of the order of 1.3 IQ points.

As a matter of fact the difference was almost exactly of that order, namely 1.28 points – but went in the opposite direction. The 1936 10-year-olds (n = 2,873) scored 100.48 and the 1949 sample (n = 3,832) scored 101.76. The mean performance above the median for each sample remained almost constant, whereas the mean for those below the respective medians rose about 2.5 points. Above the IQ of 130 there was a decrease, whereas below there was an increase.

Cattell (1950) offered three hypotheses, any of which could conceivably reconcile the adverse findings with his original prediction:
(1) There might have been a "true" decline of intelligence which was "masked" by the test's being "vulnerable to extraneous influence"

(*op. cit.*, p. 140). That is to say, some environmental influences could have operated.

(2) No real decline had occurred, because differential birth rates had been "offset by differential death, celibacy, barren marriages, etc."

(3) Education could have been "confused" with intelligence.

The third hypothesis was immediately dismissed. "Psychologists have ample factor analytic proof that their tests – though doubtless somewhat contaminated with education – are nevertheless substantially measuring innate mental capacity (*op. cit.*, p. 141)". Cattell himself opted for the first hypothesis. He pointed out that there were studies which had shown that a substantial expansion of educational facilities from one generation to another had resulted in a considerable increase in mean test performance. In the Scottish survey, the girls' mean increased by 3.2 points, as compared to only 1.4 for boys. Since there were no indications of sex-linked inheritance of intelligence, the differential change could be regarded as an outcome of improved educational opportunities for girls. The Scottish survey, as well as an American study by Tuddenham (1948), was carried out by means of conventional verbal intelligence tests, whereas Cattell employed his "culture-free" test. Therefore, the only "extraneous influence" which could be supposed to operate was test sophistication. However, since the experience of testing was on the whole the same in the 1949 as in the 1936 sample, the evidence did not leave much hope for that hypothesis. "It would, therefore, be a matter for debate whether this change (in test experience) could account for a 1.28 points of IQ increase in mean performance were it not that a peculiarity of the distribution – our second main finding – also would fit into a test sophistication explanation (*op. cit.*, p. 142)". The "second finding" referred to was that the increase was mainly limited to those in the middle or below the middle of the distribution. One could expect them to gain more from having been exposed to previous testings. But the studies referred to failed to support this explanation, as we shall see in the following section.

THE SCOTTISH SURVEYS, 1932 AND 1947

The 1932 Scottish survey of eleven-year-olds showed a low negative correlation between number of children in the family and the IQ of the tested child. The survey was repeated in 1947, sponsored by the Population Investigation Committee and the Scottish Council for Research in Education. As pointed out above, instead of a decrease in average performance the opposite was found. The score rose from an average of 34.5 to 36.7. The first Report (Scottish Council, 1949) advanced several reasons for this, most of them the same as had previously been advanced by Godfrey Thomson in his paper read to the Eugenics Society (see p. 65). In his Preface to the Report, Thomson said about the rise in mean score: "Undoubtedly this strengthens the environmental side of the argument – unless the increase is due to that 'test sophistication' spoken of in the previous paragraph; unless, that is, the environmental influence enables the children to answer the test more satisfactorily without raising their general intelligence. In the present volume we cannot prove or disprove this possibility, if indeed we ever can" (p. VIII–IX). The reader wonders how it could logically be possible to make any judgment on the development of general intelligence as a genetic entity without relying on the test instruments.

Further, the Introduction to the Report pointed out that the direction of causality, when interpreting the correlation between family size and IQ, had become less clear-cut than it appeared when the first surveys were conducted. Were intelligent parents more than the unintelligent ones trying to restrict the number of children they conceived, or did a large number of children in a family have a lowering effect upon IQ?

Another explanation for the unexpected increase was the one mentioned above, advanced by Penrose (1949), as to the effect of differential non-reproduction, i.e., the effect of low reproduction of mentally retarded. Since the Scottish survey did not include data on this, the validity of the Penrose model could not be tested.

Thomson felt that the failure to obtain confirming evidence should not lead to premature interpretations. He thought that "a genetic loss is actually going on and is merely being masked by environmental causes which can only be temporary and must be defeated in the long run by persistent selection". He went on to say: "we must examine ... every conceivable explanation which may leave open the possibility that adverse selection is still going on behind a facade of temporary improvement" (p. XII). The Darwinian tradition was strong among British psychologists.

Insofar as "masked" improvement is concerned, let us consider again the second volume of the Report mainly prepared by Maxwell (Scottish Council, 1953), wherein the social implications of the Scottish Mental Survey were brought out. The main topic in this volume was the relationship between IQ and social background, but *height* was also found to be related to both IQ and family size (cf. Maxwell, 1961). Indeed, height over the years "behaved" almost the same as IQ; that is, there was a low negative correlation between height and family size, but there was a marked increase in standing height from 1932 to 1947 (something which, by the way, has been observed in all countries, where representative data for successive age groups of school children or military inductees have been available). To say that increased height is an outcome of "height sophistication" makes no sense in rtying to save the "genetic loss" hypothesis.

US DRAFTEE IQ IN 1917 AND IN 1943

Tuddenham (1948) took advantage of the availability of test data for an experimental, representative sample of 768 American enlisted men in World War II, who after having taken the Army General Classification Test (AGCT) at induction later took a revised version of the World War I Army Alpha. The later version, however, yields very similar distribution of scores, particularly in the upper quartile.

Tuddenham found that the service men of the World War II sample surpassed the World War I norms quite considerably. The median score in World War I corresponded only to the 22nd percentile in the World War II sample. Inversely, the median for World War II corresponded to the 83rd percentile in World War I. These findings ran contrary to the predictions made by several researchers in the 1930's and 1940's, namely that there would be a decline of 3 to 4 IQ points per generation due to the longrange effect of family size being inversely related to test performance, education and socio-economic level.

Three major explanations were advanced by Tuddenham for the increased test performance:

(1) The 1943 sample had had some experience in testing during school and perhaps during their working career. Furthermore, they had taken the AGCT before the Alpha, the first being administered at the beginning of their military service and the second some time later. But increased test sophistication and practice in 1943 as compared to 1917–18 could account for only a minor portion of the increase.

(2) Improvements in public health and nutrition could have contributed. Tuddenham refers, for instance, to increased height and longevity.

(3) The 1917 population had on the average 8 years of schooling, whereas the 1943 sample had completed 10 years. When the World

War I distribution was reweighted to make it comparable with the World War II sample in terms of education, it was found that about half the increase in mean performance could be attributed to length of education. But one would expect another sizable portion to be attributable to improved quality of education.

ANNUAL SURVEYS ON SWEDISH CONSCRIPTS 1949–1953

Conscripts in the Swedish Armed Forces are required to appear before a Conscription Board before they begin their military service. From 1944 until 1950 the age of conscription was 20, and every man, apart from those who had entered military service earlier as regulars, was required to appear before a Board at the age of 20; in 1950 and for some years after, they were called up at the age of 19. Thus in 1949, two complete age cohorts were drafted. At the beginning of the 1950's the average size of a complete age cohort was close to 40,000 (cf. Husén, 1953, 1959). The conscripts made up about 95 per cent of the cohort, since some 3 to 4 per cent were regulars enrolled earlier (Husén, 1948). Only 0.3 per cent failed to appear before the Boards. Thus, data for the overwhelming majority of the males in the relevant age groups were available. (There was no point in calculating the standard errors of estimation, since entire populations were tested and not samples drawn from them.) The classification test was a group-administered intelligence test made up of some 4 to 8 categories of items with some preponderance of verbal test categories (Husén and Henricson, 1951; Husén, 1959), and was almost identical throughout the years 1949–1953. Since two age cohorts, the 19- and 20-year-olds, were tested in 1949, altogether six age groups were tested with the same test. The only changes that occurred involved a few single items that were replaced by more adequate items at the same level of difficulty. The number of items was 160 and the standard deviation was about 30. The mean scores on the test and the standard deviations were:

Year of Testing	M	SD	n
1949: 1	78.41 (20-year olds)	30.73	39,075
1949: 2	78.53 (19-year olds)	30.17	38,777
1950	79.00 (19-year olds)	29.98	38,976
1951	80.76 (19-year olds)	29.53	38,416
1952	81.70 (19-year olds)	n.a.	n.a.
1953	81.70 (19-year olds)	n.a.	n.a.

The increase in average raw score over the entire period was 3.3 points. Comparisons limited to the period when only 19-year-olds were tested yield an increase of 3.17 points over the four-year period. This is a little less than one-tenth of one standard deviation. If the same rate of increase has been obtained since then, we would expect an increase in mean performance of about 0.6 SD, a prediction that could be tested provided a representative sample of the 1974 conscripts were given the 1953 test.

A FRENCH SURVEY

L'Institut National d'Etudes Démographiques (Heuyer *et al.* 1950) in 1944 conducted a national survey in France of the intellectual level of children in primary school. A sample of almost 100,000 pupils was drawn such as to be representative of children from 6 through 12 years of age. The mosaic test, a group intelligence test constructed by René Gille, was administered. The chief purpose of the survey was to calibrate and to assess the validity of an instrument that could be used in the French schools for various purposes, not least as an aid in providing educational and vocational guidance. Evidently, the data collected provided excellent information of a kind that could only be obtained from a large and representative sample of children. Thus Henry (Heuyer *et al.* 1950, p. 47 *et seq.*) was able to carry out analyses pertaining to sex differences, social class differences, and the relationship between IQ and family size.

Henry analyzed the test scores with regard to age, sex, place of residence, and socio-economic background. Of particular interest in this connection is, of course, the correlation between the number of children in the family and the test scores. The average score decreased very little from 1 to 2 children, more from 2 to 5 children, and rather little from 5 to 8. But the decreasing mean score by number of children was, as in the case of the British surveys noted above, for the most part consistent and significant. This was so particularly among lower class groups, such as farm workers and urban manual workers, although among professionals and intellectuals there was no consistent decline at all, the only-child average being about the same as in families with 6 children. The white-collar workers ("*les employés*") showed a moderate decline, while there was considerable decline throughout among manual workers, whether in rural or urban areas (see Table 4).

TABLE 4: *Mean Score on Intelligence Test by Parental Occupation and Number of Children in Family in the 1944 INED Survey*

Number of Children	Farmers, Growers	Farm Workers	White Collar Rural Workers	Manual Urban Workers	White Collar Urban Workers	Middle Level Management	Professionals, Intellectuals	Total Sample
1	93,6	100,5	110,0	107,3	111,9	113,5	125,8	105,9
2	94,4	98,7	106,8	104,9	111,2	112,6	124,9	104,7
3	92,0	95,1	101,6	100,8	108,6	111,3	120,1	101,6
4	88,9	92,5	100,8	97,7	105,5	110,5	121,9	99,1
5	86,3	88,2	96,9	93,2	103,1	106,9	122,4	95,7
6	86,6	82,7	89,8	91,7	98,8	108,8	126,7	93,5
7	84,0	83,8	85,8	90,4	97,6	102,8	119,3	91,5
8	83,3	80,5	90,4	87,6	98,1	100,8	109,5	90,4
9	81,7	77,2	78,1	83,9	94,8	94,1	101,3	85,9

Source: Heuyer et al., 1950.

In discussing the outcomes of his analyses, Henry suggested that the differential relationship between family size and intelligence according to social strata could be accounted for more by social factors than by hereditary influences. The economic burden of having many children could be expected to lower the cultural level of the home and thereby influence the mental development of the children. The rapport between children and parents could be substantially diminished by the number of children, whereby a negative influence would be exerted on intellectual development. Henry concluded by saying: *"Dans l'état actuel de nos connaissances, il parait donc prudent de réserver notre jugement. L'existence d'une corrélation négative entre niveau socio-économique et fécondité est peut-être le seul cause de la corrélation entre dimension de la famille et niveau intellectuel des enfants"* (op. cit., p. 96).

RECENT STUDIES

The World Population Conference in Rome in 1954 based its proceedings upon the extensive research on family size and intelligence that had been going on over the decade after World War II. As we have seen above, an enormous amount of survey data had been collected in England and Scotland through several sources under the auspices of the Eugenics Society. In 1954 Henry published his analyses of French survey data from 1944 (Henry, 1954). In 1956 Anne Anastasi conducted a critical review of the relevant literature in the field up to that date and very succinctly brought out the methodological issues and suggested as well new avenues of research, one of which would be longitudinal studies. Higgins *et al.* (1962) made an ambitious attempt to follow her advice. In an article titled "Intelligence and Family Size: A Paradox Resolved" they reported a massive study conducted at the Minnesota State School and Hospital where a sample of 1016 families had been followed up for at least a generation. The "paradox" is, of course, the increase of IQ from one generation to another in spite of the correlation of the order of $-.2$ to $-.3$ between family size and IQ of the children.

Higgins and his associates took as their starting point a study conducted by Willoughby and Coogan (1940), who had followed a group of high school graduates for 12 years after graduation and found that if everybody was included (that is, even those who did not "produce" any children at all) the high IQ group "produced" more children than the low IQ group, something that was not the case if the individuals without children (who had been left out in practically all previous surveys) were not considered. The Willoughby and Coogan study was based on a small and select sample and was therefore open to criticism as to the generalizability of the results.

Higgins and his co-workers (1962) had information on IQ both for parents in 1,016 cases and for their 2,039 children. The mean IQ's were:

Mothers	103.2
Fathers	100.7
Girls	107.7
Boys	105.0

Part of the difference between generations was due to age; the parents had been tested on the average at the age of 15 and their children at age 9. The correlations between members of the same family tended to be of the magnitude obtained in many previous studies. Thus, the sibling correlation was .52, husband-wife .33, mother-child .45, and father-child .43.

The correlation between number of children and IQ was found to be —.30, which was consistent with findings in previous studies. The mean IQ did not differ considerably with the number of children per family in the range of 1 to 5, but then dropped quite a lot for families with over 5 children. But when the single and non-reproductive siblings of the parents were included, the negative correlation disappeared altogether. "The higher reproductive rates of those in the lower IQ groups *who are parents* (italics mine) is offset by the large proportion of their siblings who never marry or who fail to reproduce when married" (*op. cit.*, pp. 89–90).

One year later Bajema (1962) published a study based on 1,144 Whites born in 1916 and 1917 in Kalamazoo, Michigan, for 979 of whom he had obtained life histories. Bajema pointed out: "It is desirable ... to investigate reproductive differentials in a variety of human societies at frequent intervals in order to assess the biological consequences of various social practices" (*op. cit.*, p. 175). He took advantage of the criticism advanced by Penrose and others at the beginning of the 1950's that previous survey research had failed to take into account variables such as (1) number of offspring per fertile individual, (2) proportions of non-reproductive individuals, (3) mortality rates up to the end of child-bearing period, and (4) generation length. Each of these factors could, considering the low correlation, have a substantial influence upon the relationship between family size and IQ.

The average number of offspring per individual in the parental generation at the various IQ levels was:

IQ	M	N
120–	2.60	82
105–119	2.24	282
95–104	2.02	318
80– 94	2.46	267
69– 79	1.50	30
Total	2.24	979

This table clearly supports the explanation given by Higgins and his associates (1962) for the "paradox" of IQ failing to deteriorate according to expectation. It is simply that the conclusion drawn from the previous surveys was premature. It was based upon inadequate data since, among other things, the non-reproductive individuals in the parent generation were not included.

The recommendation by Bajema that reproductive differentials be studied at frequent intervals and not be regarded as constant over many generations has been further reinforced by Benjamin (1966), who points out that according to later Censuses in England the fertility of Social Class I (professionals) had increased from previous Censuses and was equal to that of the other social classes. Thus a strong upward fertility among the more educated could be observed on both sides of the Atlantic, something that was not anticipated in the forecasts of deteriorating intelligence in the 1930's and 1940's.

METHODOLOGICAL ISSUES AND CONCLUSIONS

As mentioned above, the problem area labeled "family size and intelligence", somewhat deceptively referred to as "differential fertility and intelligence" by many researchers (cf. p. 74), was subjected to scrutiny by Anne Anastasi (1956) shortly after the World Population Conference in Rome. She advanced ample support for her statement that careful analyses of the problem "have revealed that it is far more complex – both methodologically and theoretically – than was originally supposed" (*op. cit.*, p. 187). The basic concepts that had been used in the research, even those, such as "fertility" or "family size" that seemingly were easy to define, were unclear in many investigations. The first large surveys did not take into account that single adults or married adults without children were not included. Nor that family size takes on a different meaning in an intact family from that in a broken home where one parent is missing from the household.

As Thomson pointed out in introducing the 1947 Scottish survey, the direction of cause and effect *might* be the reverse of that hypothesized by most investigators. Thus, a rationale could be advanced for the hypothesis that many children in the family might adversely affect intellectual development, particularly in lower class families. This would seem more plausible indeed than to hypothesize that parental intelligence determines how large they make their family. It becomes even more plausible when one takes into account that most investigators have related the size of the family not to the intellectual performance of the parents but to that of the *children*.

By way of summing up, five assumptions on which the conclusions of a deteriorating intelligence have been based are found upon examination to be incorrect or beset with important limitations.

(1) The prediction of a declining intelligence is based on the assumption of a *universal* negative correlation between family size and IQ in the "civilized" countries, a negative relationship that will prevail for many future generations. It is true, that demographic data in some European countries before 1940 showed a negative correlation between social status and number of children in the family. Lower class families tended to have more children than middle or upper class families, where birth control was more frequent. But, as was pointed out at the World Population Conference in Rome in 1954 (United Nations, 1955), the trend in several countries had already been reversed by then to the effect that high scoring children tended to come from larger families than those who scored around the average. The French intelligence survey of 1944 with a follow-up in 1951 focused among other things on the relationship between family size and IQ. It was found that the variability between social strata tended to be of the same order of magnitude as that between families with different numbers of children within the same stratum. It was also found that the score decreased much more by number of children in rural or working class families than in professional and intellectual families. Thus, the negative correlation was particularly marked in the lower class families (Henry, 1954, p. 55). Similar findings had been reported from British surveys.

(2) The negative correlation between the IQ of the child and the number of his siblings is not the same as the correlation between the mean *parental* IQ and the number of offspring. It is another matter

that mean parental IQ is close to the mean for the offspring. Before the beginning of the 1960's no comparative study of such correlations had been conducted in Europe or the United States.

(3) The causal relationship between IQ and "fertility" (incorrectly defined as the number of children in families *with* children) can, as was pointed out above, be conceived in a reverse way. A child born into a family with many, closely spaced, siblings cannot obtain the same individual care and personal interest as a child born into a family with only one or two siblings. Research on pre-school education at home and at school conducted during the last two decades has given us evidence how material and cultural poverty affect children during their first year of life, not least with regard to their cognitive development. Thus, the fact that there is a clear-cut negative correlation between family size and IQ in lower class families, and not in more socially privileged strata, is an indication that the negative correlation found is chiefly an effect of environmental conditions in large families.

(4) Studies of the relationship between fertility and IQ have not, until recently, taken into account adults who did *not* reproduce. One also has to consider other demographic factors, such as mortality rate and generation length. Follow-up studies are the only ones that can take all these factors into account. Such investigations provide evidence that the number of non-reproductive individuals in the various social strata and IQ brackets plays a decisive role in accounting for the correlation between family size and IQ of the children.

(5) The whole conception that a negative correlation between child-IQ and number of siblings must lead to an intellectual decline, even to "bankruptcy", is based on the assumption that the tests measure practically only "inherited intelligence". The evidence we have both from extensive surveys and from intensive studies of small groups of children tells us that this assumption is tenable only to a limited extent.

In her review of the research up to the mid-fifties, Anastasi (1956) pointed out that conclusive answers to the many questions raised in connection with studies of differential fertility could be provided by longitudinal studies:

"Ideally, such investigations should begin with the testing of young people prior to their educational and vocational differentiation, i.e., after all have completed a uniform period of required schooling. Preferably the tests should consist of a differential aptitude battery yielding a profile of scores rather than a single global measure. The subjects should be followed up until all or nearly all of their families are completed. Age of both parents at the birth of their first and last child should be recorded. Data should also be kept on deaths, unmarried persons, and childless marriages. Information should likewise be gathered regarding occupation, income level, and amount of subsequent education for each member of the group. It would also be of interest to obtain indices of social mobility, such as changes in occupational, educational, or income level within the subject's own life, as well as differences between his status and that of his parents" (*op. cit.*, p. 206).

Since her article was written at least two longitudinal studies, referred to above, have been conducted and have come a long way toward resolving the "paradox" that emerged from the cross-sectional survey research in the 1940's (Higgins *et al.*, 1962; Bajema, 1962). The data collected in 1938 in the city of Malmoe for some 1,500 ten-year-olds who have since then been followed up are a close fit to the ideal for a research design outlined in the quotation from Anastasi. The only exception is that the group intelligence test, although providing both a verbal and a nonverbal subscore, cannot provide an aptitude profile (Husén, 1969). One should in this context also study the long-range cognitive development in different social strata. The model of heredity-environment interaction advanced by Scarr-Salapatek (1971) was presented above (p. 21); according to this model genetic differences will have a stronger influence on observed cognitive differences among children from upper strata than on those from lower strata, because the latter are hampered by the deprivational conditions in which they grow up. This would mean that in a society where health services, nutritional conditions and educational facilities are improved, those who are below a certain threshold of deprivation will be the ones to particularly benefit. The outcome would be that the average level of cognitive competence is raised.

As a preparation for the World Population Conference in Rome in September of 1954, UNESCO convened a group of scientists within its Division of Applied Social Sciences who were asked to consider the matter of the "alleged decline in the average intelligence of national populations" and the failed predictions "as to the rate of such a decline". The group, consisting largely of geneticists and demographers, arrived at the following factors as explaining the "discrepancy between the pessimistic predictions and the objective findings", such as those from the Scottish survey of 1947 (Scottish Council, 1949, 1953):

"(a) The tendency for greater fertility to be found at lower economic levels, and the accompanying differences in educational opportunities open to children of larger and smaller families respectively.

(b) The lack of any one-to-one correspondence between the test intelligence of parents and that of children.

(c) The great overlapping of abilities between different sub-groups in the population.

(d) The failure of nearly all surveys to take account of childless members of the community.

(e) The increasing tendency for individuals to find their mates outside their own groups.

(f) The effect of social mobility" (United Nations, 1955).

A CONCLUDING REMARK

We have at some length dealt with the research, and the debate in its wake, on the long-range effect of differential fertility on the size of the pool of talent. In the 1930's psychologists were quick in drawing conclusions from available survey data. The repetition of surveys in the 1940's made researchers aware of the methodological intricacies in conducting studies in this area. By the time of the World Population Conference in the 1950's the methodological snags were succinctly summed up by Anne Anastasi (1956) who advanced a rationale for longitudinal studies, which were conducted in the 1960's and lended no support to the speedy conclusions in the 1930's of a shrinking pool of talent reflected in a lowering of the mean IQ in the general population. It has been worthwhile writing up the story of the evolving research also from the point of view that it illuminates the role played by implied ideologies, in this case for or against eugenic measures that would enhance IQ. Considering our present knowledge a decline in mean intellectual performance is not in sight, on the contrary it seems to rise.

CHAPTER 5

ABILITY, EDUCATION, AND ECONOMIC SUCCESS

"HUMAN RESOURCES AS THE WEALTH OF NATIONS"

Since this book is focused on the availability of a pool of talent, it would seem appropriate to discuss briefly the broader social and economic implications of the concept, using recent thinking on the economics of education as a starting point. The heading of this introductory section has therefore been borrowed from Harbison's (1973) book of the same name. Harbison deals mainly with the less developed countries, but the idea of the contribution of the formal educational system to economic growth applies, of course, with different degrees of forcefulness to all national economies. His basic premise is simply that "human resources are the ultimate basis of the wealth of nations. From this perspective, the goals of development are the maximum possible utilization of human beings in productive activity and the fullest possible development of skills, knowledge, and capacities of the labor force. If these goals are pursued, then others such as economic growth, higher levels of living, and more equitable distribution of income are thought to be the likely consequences" (Harbison, 1973, Preface).

It would be wrong to convey the impression that Harbison looks upon the formal and informal educational systems, together constituting what he calls the "learning system", only as instruments geared to economic growth, and hence to producing in due proportions a labor force having the adequate skills and knowledge. He also emphasizes their role in enriching human life and in enabling the individual to participate more fully in the life of the community and in public affairs by making him aware if the problems which beset the community, humanity, and the world at large. But being an economist and dealing with problems pertaining mainly to the less developed countries his main concern is the "relationship between education and the world of work" (*op. cit.*, p. 54). This means, then, that he takes the so-called manpower approach to educational policy and planning. As far as the industrialized countries are concerned, this approach had its heyday at the beginning of the 1960's in the wake of the first OECD Policy Conference on Economic Growth and Investment in Education (OECD, 1962). By investing in education one would more or less automatically boost the economy.

The fact that in most West European countries and in the United States expenditures on education increased about three times as rapidly as did the GNP did not in the 1960's cause any particular concern. The costs of school education have in most of the advanced countries been rising by some 15 per cent per year, and education has come to compete even more acutely with other urgent public needs. The boosting of formal education, conceived of by most economists as an entity measured by number of school years (see, e.g., Harbison and Myers, 1964), did not achieve, however, the results hoped for at the beginning of the 1960's.

According to a presentation by Machlup (1973) at the fall meeting in 1973 of the US National Academy of Education, the growth rate of the entire "knowledge industry" since 1958, when he finished the data collection for the first edition of his book on the production and distribution of knowledge (Machlup, 1962), has been 9 per cent a year.

Yet, the hope many held at the beginning of the 1960's that expanding educational opportunities would create equality in participation in education did not materialize to the extent that they had envisaged (cf. OECD, 1970; Jencks, 1972). Progressive educational policy to promote greater equity of participation to the benefit of the socially disadvantaged in society, appeared at least partly to have failed (OECD, 1971c). Moreover, it was hard to prove any positive relationship between investment in education and the growth of GNP (e.g. Becker, 1964).

But the educational system tries to pursue goals which are not accessible to cost-benefit analyses. To enter upon an analysis of the objectives of the educational system in this context would take us far afield. So let us confine ourselves to noting that those concerned with the role of school education in modern, rapidly changing society unanimously endorse as one main objective of the school the enrichment of the life of the individual in the social context he grows up in, thus helping him to realize his own potentialities for structuring his interests and to become aware of his community and the rest of humanity.

Both formal and non-formal education is inextricably intertwined with the encompassing social system. It is wrong to conceive of school education as a "separate" system which "prepares" the individual for the labor market. As a matter of fact, the differences between pupils in terms of competence achieved are accounted for mainly by social background and only to a rather modest extent by the quality of formal schooling as such. (Coleman, 1966, 1973; Plowden, 1967; Husén, 1967; Comber and Keeves, 1973). This problem has been dramatized by the debate ensuing from Christopher Jencks' book *Inequality*, published in 1972. He concludes that the character, i.e., the quality, of an individual's education seems to have an almost negligible "effect" on his occupational career and earnings. What matters in terms of occupational status are credentials. These are dependent upon the *amount* of education, i.e., the number of years of schooling. The amount of schooling in turn is closely related to family background. To separate the importance of school quality from social status is very difficult, simply because of the intercorrelations between social status, area of residence, choice of school, and outcome in terms of pupil performance. The methodological debate ensuing from *Inequality* indicates the intricacy, not to say the impossibility, by means of cross-sectional data to separate school effects from influences exercised by the home and other agents in the larger social setting.

By and large, the available survey research suggests that the most important input factor is the social composition of the enrollment and that school resources in terms of quality of curricula, text-books, teacher competence, etc., play a secondary role in accounting for cognitive *differences* between pupils within schools as well as between schools. This was highlighted by the multivariate analyses of achievements in the multinational evaluation of educational systems conducted by the International Association for the Evaluation of Educational Achievements (IEA). The total home background effects were compared to the total direct school effects as 0.3 to 0.2 on the 10-year-old level and 0.4 to 0.3 on the 14-year-old level (Coleman, 1973). The huge gap in mean performance in Science and Reading between industrialized and non-industrialized countries can be accounted for largely by differences in the socio-cultural and economic matrix within which the various systems are operating.

This does not, however, mean that schools or school resources are "unimportant" or "don't make any difference". The "effect" referred to in Jencks' and other studies is assessed by the portion of the between-pupil variance which is explained by school resources, a portion that can be quite substantial in school-oriented subjects like Science.

Educational planners, particularly those with a background in administration and economics, tend to conceive of the role of an educational system mainly in terms of how it succeeds in developing human resources for the economy. This viewpoint overlooks certain conditions that begin to prevail in a modern industrialized society on the threshold of the post-industrial era. According to surveys in the United States cited by Thurow (1972), about two thirds of the workers had acquired their current job skills through more or less informal on-the-job training. In the society of today the traditional institutions of formal schooling no longer have a monopoly on providing certain skills and knowledge. This will become even more evident in the post-industrial society. The informal system through mass media, evening courses, correspondence instruction, and in-plant training has become more and more "information-rich" and powerful. The formal system more and more has to limit its role to making people "trainable".

Regardless of whether one accepts the propositions of those who have studied the national and individual economic return of "investment" in education, the fact remains that the "knowledge industry" (Machlup) in Europe as well as the United States will proceed to grow in the foreseeable future, even if the growth rate may not be as rapid as it was during 1960's. Unfortunately, we do not have European studies comparable in comprehensiveness and thoroughness to the one conducted by Fritz Machlup (1962) in the United States, and which has been brought up to date by utilizing the 1970 Census data. But there is ample reason to project (with some time lag) the same trend in Western Europe. The enrollment explosion at the secondary and tertiary levels of the educational systems has hit Europe later than it did the United States, which accounts for the fact that the enrollment growth has been relatively more rapid in Europe during the beginning of the 1970's and can be expected to remain so for the rest of the decade. Since the development in Europe in terms of sheer size of the "knowledge industry" can be expected to be parallel (with some time lag), it is of interest to review briefly the US situation.

Machlup (1973) defines the "knowledge industry" as education, research and development, media of communication, information machines, and information servicing. Formal education in the United States in 1958 accounted for about 44 per cent of the total output of the knowledge industry, which corresponded to about 13 per cent of the GNP. Using another approach, the occupational one, whereby the number of individuals employed full-time in education was taken into account, the output of education amounted to more than 14 per cent of the GNP. Since 1958 enrollment has increased; in 1970 60 per cent of the 18–21 year olds were in higher education, as compared to 34 per cent in 1960. Furthermore, the unit cost (per student per year) has increased considerably, which means the growth rate in expenditures on education is probably considerably higher than the 9 per cent given by Machlup for the entire knowledge industry.

To adopt another approach in measuring the growth of formal education: OECD (1971a) has collated enrollment statistics in higher education in its member countries for the period 1950–1967. The increased enrollment in absolute numbers can be put into perspective by relating these numbers to the total population, and by comparing percentages of the total age group(s) enrolled in higher education, in 1950 and 1965. The total number of enrolled students in higher education per 1,000 of the total population increased in the following way in the United States, Japan, and some West European countries:

Country	1950	1965
United States	15.1	28.6
Japan	4.8	11.1
Denmark	4.8	10.9
Finland	4.2	10.3
France	4.2	10.3
Sweden	3.1	10.0
Italy	5.1	8.3
Norway	2.8	7.8
Germany	3.6	7.2

There are also great variations between countries in terms of the proportion of the *eligible graduates* from upper secondary school who enter institutions of higher education. In Germany, Sweden, France and Denmark, by the middle of the 1960's between 90 and 100 per cent of the graduates went on to higher education, whereas there were only some 40–50 per cent in the United States and Norway, and as small a proportion as 20 per cent in Japan.

The number of students of relevant enrollment age in per cent of the *total age groups* were:[1]

Country	1950	1965
United States	19.0	28.1
Japan	6.2	13.3
Sweden	3.8	12.6
France	—	11.6
Denmark	4.6	10.2
Finland	4.1	10.1
Norway	3.3	8.0
Germany	3.7	6.3

U68 in its task of drawing up an organizational blueprint for the Swedish system of higher education adopts the manpower approach in planning a great many programs of study which will be more geared to occupational sectors and sub-sectors than has so far been the case. This, of course, does not square with the overall conception of the relationship between the economy and the educational system that Thurow (1972) and other economists have, namely that the economy attempts to adapt its requirements to the available competence in terms of general education and not vice versa. One has ample reason to question an approach that was *en vogue* at the beginning of the 1960's and after that has been applied with so little success in countries with quite different economic and social orders.

But the main point here is that regardless of whether or not one takes a systematic manpower approach in estimating the demand for upper secondary and higher education, one can safely forecast some increase in total enrollment for the next 20 to 25 years. In the first place, those who are in the system or are about to enter it can be expected to take advantage of the broadened opportunities at the secondary and tertiary levels. Difficulties in finding employment in one's particular area of preparation can be expected to offset this tendency

[1] The forcefulness of the "explosion" that has taken place can be illustrated by citing the enrollment statistics for higher education in Sweden from the Royal Commission on Higher Education, known as U68 (sou, 1973). The number of first-year enrolled students at institutions of higher education grew from about 2,000 in 1940–41 to 26,000 in 1970–71. During the same period the total number of full-time students at these institutions has increased from 11,000 to 125,000.

U68 adopted two approaches in trying to project the size of the system of higher education by 1980. A "flow-analysis" has been conducted under the overall assumption of an unchanged structure of the entire educational system. The other approach has been a manpower analysis based on data from the 1960 and 1965 censuses and on projected needs of the various sectors of the economy.

only to a limited extent. Secondly, we can expect a greater age spread in enrollment inasmuch as an increasing number of individuals may after completion of secondary education prefer to obtain work experience before going on to further education. Many of those who re-enter the system have rather precisely defined goals (not least the "marketable" ones) for their education in mind. Thirdly, within an expanding system of "recurrent" education many adults can be expected to enroll for short periods in order to take specific courses which either fit into their career pattern or are part of their leisure time interests.

In a system of recurrent education the institutions of higher learning become integrated into a larger system of life-long learning, which has thus far emerged outside these institutions under the auspices of adult education organizations, business, industry and public administration. After an era of enrollment explosion such a system will contribute to bridging the "education gap" between generations. It can also promote flexibility in terms of providing maximum freedom for the individual to pursue a life-long educational career compatible with his occupational bent (Bengtsson, 1972).

IQ, EDUCATION, AND ECONOMIC SUCCESS

The debate in recent years on what "causes" individual differences in adult careers has been somewhat confused. No wonder, then, that the policy recommendations ensuing from various major studies have been contradictory. For a long time the liberal equality-of-opportunity principle (to use Charles Frankel's expression: the "corrective egalitarianism") was thought to be an effective way both to eliminate poverty and to bring about greater equity in life careers, particularly in terms of economic success. To remove economic and geographical barriers that prevented young people of lower class or rural background from getting access to advanced education would be to provide individuals with equal chances, irrespective of social background, of reaching high status positions in society. Organizations like OECD devoted considerable resources to studying how ability as a national asset was to be taken care of and to devising strategies that would bring about enhanced equality of opportunity for education at the upper secondary and university levels. The Kungälv Conference (Halsey, 1961) can be regarded as a landmark in these endeavors. But, contrary to the expectations, the surveys of educational participation conducted by OECD itself at the end of the 1960's tended to show that, in spite of the tremendous enrollment expansion, the disparities between social strata had not been considerably reduced; in some cases they had even increased (OECD, 1970, 1971c). J. R. Gass of the Center for Educational Research and Innovation (CERI), pointing out the "disillusion" as to what education could do, concluded that "big increases in education in the 1950s and 1960s brought about only marginal advances in equality of opportunity" (Husén, 1972, p. 7).

During the latter part of the 1960s several surveys cast further doubt on the proposition that education could act as a "great equalizer". The Coleman Report of 1966, the Plowden Report of 1967, the Blau and Duncan analysis (1967) of US Census Bureau data from 1962, and the IEA report on mathematics (Husén, 1967), all tended to show the home background to be of overwhelming importance in accounting for both between-school and between-student differences in achievement in key school subjects. Recent IEA surveys covering other subject areas than mathematics seem by and large to confirm this, even though in some cases, as in Science, the amount of variation explained by school factors tends to be greater than for skill subjects such as reading (Comber and Keeves, 1973; Thorndike, 1973). The 1960's also witnessed a renaissance of research on pre-school development, which focused on the differences between children in their ability to absorb what was offered to them then, and later when they began formal schooling. The differences that emerged during their formal school career were rather moderate in comparison to those that existed when they had entered school. This, of course, also contributed to discounting the role played by the school in providing career opportunities.

But findings from surveys like the ones mentioned above have been very differently interpreted, not only depending upon the "ideology" of the researcher but also owing to the lack of conceptual and methodological rigor which has prevailed in this so politically sensitive field. In his much-debated study *Inequality*, which carries the subtitle "A Reassessment of the Effect of Family and Schooling in America", Christopher Jencks builds up a massive skepticism towards those policies giving education a pivotal role in equalizing life careers or at least in lifting those who are born into poverty. In the concluding chapter he says: "There seem to be three reasons why school reform cannot make adults more equal. First, children seem to be far more influenced by what happens at home than by what happens in school. They may also be more influenced by what happens on the streets and by what they see on television. Second, reformers have very little control over those aspects of school life that affect children. Reallocating resources, reassigning pupils, and rewriting the curriculum seldom change the way teachers and students actually treat each other minute by minute. Third, even when a school exerts an unusual influence on children, the resulting changes are not likely to persist into adulthood" (pp. 255–6).

In an article titled "IQ and the US Class Structure" which we have briefly dealt with in Chapter 2, Samuel Bowles and Herbert Gintis (1973) strongly challenge the notion of IQ being important to economic success. The main target of their criticism is the notion that "the poor are poor because they are intellectually incompetent; their incompetence is particularly intractable because it is rooted in the genetic structure inherited from their poor and also intellectually deficient parents" (*op. cit.*, p. 65). But they also challenge the notion that "social classes sort themselves out on the basis of innate individual capacity to cope successfully in the social environment". This implies that the modern liberal social policy according to which progressive social welfare measures can "gradually reduce and eliminate social class differences" and inequalities of opportunity is unsound. They set out to show that IQ by no means is such a strong determinant of occupational status and social mobility as many social scientists seem to think.

In order to prove their thesis that social class background and not IQ is the important contributor to economic success, Bowles and Gintis took advantage of three sets of data: (1) The US Census Current Population Survey in 1962, whereof they limited themselves to data for Whites 25 to 34 years old from non-farm background and in the experienced labor force; (2) The National Opinion Research Center survey of veterans (for whom child IQ and adult IQ according to the Armed Forces Qualification Test have been compared), and (3) The California Guidance Study. Economic success was measured by average income and the social prestige of occupation according to Duncan (1961). Education was measured by number of years of schooling. Social class was measured as a weighted sum of parental education, father's occupational status and father's income.

The correlations between economic success defined by income and the other variables under scrutiny were:

"Economic success" and IQ   .52
"Economic success" and level of education[1]   .63
"Economic success" and social class   .55

[1] defined by number of years of schooling

The correlations obtained are on the whole comparable with those arrived at in other studies (Husén, 1969). IQ, number of years of schooling, and social class seem to predict adult career to about the same extent, with level of education tending to be the best single predictor. The authors then try to do what other investigators have also tried, that is to "derive numerical estimates of the independent contributors of each of the separate but correlated influences (social class background, childhood IQ, years of schooling, adult IQ) on economic success" (*op. cit.*, pp. 71–2). The technique employed is the linear regression analysis, which is supposed to give the correlation between each of the predictors and adult economic success with other predictors being kept constant. If social class and education are kept under control, a beta coefficient of only .13 is obtained between IQ and economic success as compared to beta coefficients of .56 and .46 for level of education and social class respectively. It should, however, be pointed out that by regressing out *adult* IQ some of the effect of formal schooling is also taken out, because amount of formal schooling is correlated with IQ changes. Those with further schooling gain substantially in comparison with those who leave school after having completed the mandatory period (Husén, 1951b). It is not strictly justified to use adult IQ as a predictor when it can be shown that it is to a considerable extent affected by the amount of formal schooling the individual has had.

The standardized coefficient of regression between level of education and economic success turned out to be .56 with adult IQ being regressed out. The conclusion that "cognitive differences account for a negligible part of schooling's influence on economic success" (*op. cit.*, p. 72) is hardly warranted. Schooling is supposed to create cognitive differences, and it evidently succeeds in doing so. It has, for instance, a differential effect on adult IQ. The authors are so eager to prove that IQ has a non-significant influence *per se* on social career that they seemingly fail to take into account that most intelligence tests are validated against scholastic success. This means then that if one regresses out education one also to a considerable extent takes out the "effect" of IQ. IQ at the age of 10 and income at age 35 were by no means insignificantly related to each other within each social stratum in the Malmö study (Husén, 1969, p. 158; Bulcock *et al.*, 1974), but the same overall conclusion was arrived at as that by Bowles and Gintis: "The pervasive factor for success in terms of income seems to be family background" (p. 159). Both amount of formal education and cognitive abilities as measured by IQ tests given at an early stage of the school career are also of importance, but not of the same magnitude as social class.

On the basis of experience gained from various large-scale surveys one can question the adequacy of the multiple regression technique in assessing the relative "effect" of schooling on certain criteria when only cross-sectional and not longitudinal data are available. Bowles and Gintis (*op. cit.*, p. 78) define causal relation as the "partial derivate of one variable with respect to another, namely the effect of a change in one variable on another, holding constant all other relevant variables". Apart from the fact that "all other relevant variables" might not be under control, simply because they are not measured, the disentanglement by means of multiple regression analysis applied to cross-sectional data is based on assumptions of doubtful validity (cf. Peaker, 1974; Coleman, 1973).

Thus, the single-equation regression technique has certain serious limitations, as pointed out by Coleman (1973), Lewin (1972), Mood (1970), and others. Furthermore, there are important measurement problems. IQ as defined by performance on intelligence tests by and large seems to have the same long-range predictive value regarding educational career as early teacher ratings of a child's scholastic ability. This is, of course, not surprising considering the fact that most intelligence tests have been validated against teacher ratings, school marks and scholastic attainments in general. Therefore, the attempt to "keep education under control" in analyzing the relationship between IQ and adult career measures results in, as was pointed out above, that quite a lot of the effect of IQ is being removed.

The criterion of equality that Jencks (1972) and his associates have employed is distribution of adult earnings, and this is referred to as "economic success". Apart from the fact that even this criterion – e.g., due to the large age spread – has not been used in such a way as to reflect the life income of the individuals included in the analyses, it has not sufficiently been emphasized in the debate that has followed publication of the book that other criteria could also have been considered, such as social mobility, status ratings, expressed satisfaction with occupation, etc.

Anyhow, Jencks arrives at the following conclusion: "Economic success seems to depend on varieties of luck and on-the-job competence that are only moderately related to family background, schooling, or scores on standardized tests" (*op. cit.*, p. 8). Thus one cannot eliminate poverty just by improving the schools or providing greater equality in access to them. "Fundamental changes" in the economic institutions, such as increased tax progression and legislation putting a floor under minimum income, are required. The findings from the study have been interpreted by some who are concerned about the rising costs of education as justifying a limitation of educational expenditures.

But Jencks' assertion that social background contributes very little to one's life success as measured by one's economic career deserves to be challenged on two counts. In the first place, it runs contrary to findings from other studies. Secondly, the methodological ground is somewhat swampy. This weakness, it should be emphasized, is shared by most of the survey research so far conducted in this field.

With reference to the first objection one could cite the present author's own follow-up study of some 1,500 ten-year-olds (Husén, 1969). Income at age 35 was related to social class and IQ at age 10 and to number of years of formal schooling in between; income was found to be highly related to social class and *within* social class significantly to amount of formal schooling. There was a considerable difference of spread of income between the social classes, the standard deviation being 3–4 times as large in the upper as in the lower-lower class (Husén, 1969, p. 156).

In his review of Jencks' book Levin (1972) points out that conclusions regarding the relative importance of social background and of schooling are partly a matter of interpretation of data. The conflict between Jencks' findings and those of other researchers to some extent merely reflects subjective judgments as to which magnitudes are important and which are not. He also points out that the most serious discrepancy between the Jencks study and others refers to the total amount of variance in earnings that is accounted for by schooling, social background, and IQ. Jencks arrives at a total of some 15 per cent, whereas other studies have found as much as 30 to 50 per cent (e.g., Coleman, 1973). Levin indicates various reasons for the low portion of adult earnings accounted for by factors that *prima facie* appear to be so important as social background and formal education.

Jencks has not adjusted income to differences in cost of living between various regions in the United States. This would account for some of the unexplained variance. But more serious is his failure to take note of the correlation between age and income, which would account for even more. Non-cognitive factors in the attitudinal or affective domain that can be expected to relate to both social background and schooling have not been taken into account. On the whole, the measures used to assess the effects of background and schooling are so crude that there is not much justification for the conclusion that when these factors do not show up in the analyses they are of little or no importance.

On top of this there are certain snags inherent in the analytic technique employed. The causal ordering of the variables in regression analyses conducted on cross-sectional data is a most crucial one. There is obviously a strong logic when it comes to a multivariate analysis, where schooling and test scores obtained during schooling are among the independent variables, to enter social background variables first in the regression equation. It can be argued that these are "at work" before schooling can begin to affect the child (cf. Peaker, 1974). But by taking out the background variance first, one also takes out the common variance between background and schooling. The technique is also built upon assumptions of linear relationships and normal distributions which as far as social background variables are concerned are seldom satisfied.

CONCLUDING REMARKS

Advanced education has expanded at an exponential rate during the last few decades and can be expected to go on expanding well into the turn of the century, even though the rate might slow down. An annual increase of 15 per cent of expenditures for education has been justified in the 1960's not only as a consumer commodity but also as an investment with a high rate of return both to the individual and to society. Even though the simplistic idea of education as boosting the economy has been seriously questioned in recent years, trained intelligence has become a commodity commanding rising prices on the market and tends to be allocated to influential and rewarding positions in both the capitalist and the socialist economies.

In spite of a policy of increased equality of educational opportunity, surveys conducted in recent years indicate that inequalities of adult earnings are of the same order of magnitude as they were some decades ago. This has brought some researchers to question not only the liberal conception of equality of opportunity but also the role played in individual careers by cognitive differences, be they expressed in IQ terms or by number of years of formal schooling. The most radical criticism maintains that the simple correlations one finds between IQ or schooling on the one hand and adult economic success on the other are due not to genuine cognitive differences but to the class stratification system in which formal schooling and the credentials ensuing from it serves as a legitimizing agent in maintaining a hierarchy in the labor market which basically is a social class hierarchy. Scrutiny of the evidence, however, does not support the contention, for instance, that IQ measured at the beginning of the school career is of negligible importance for adult success. Other aspects of the question are still open, inasmuch as the surveys that have so far been conducted are almost entirely based on cross-sectional and not on longitudinal data. With the former type of data it is extremely difficult to disentangle the unique influence of the various differentiating factors related to social background, child IQ, and school attainments. Studies that are based on longitudinal data suggest that IQ is related to adult earnings within the various social strata as well as to adult mobility between these strata.

CHAPTER 6

INHERITED DIVERSITY, EQUALITY, AND MERITOCRACY

EQUALITY AND GENETIC DIVERSITY

The nature-nurture controversy, as could be seen from the brief account in Chapter 2, has been beset by many confusions which have barred further clarification of the issues and have impeded empirical research. For example, the heriditary component of behavioural traits must be *inferred from a process of development* that is not directly accessible to measurement.

In a recent book Dobzhansky (1973) has attempted to bridge the gap between social philosophy and biology in the conception of the heredity-environment issue. He spells out the biological implications of the social philosophy of equality as well as the social implications of certain biological conditions behind human diversity. Dobzhansky starts out by underlining that equality should not be confused with identity. The same applies to inequality and diversity. Equality is a social and not a biological concept. Another confusion stems from the use of the word "determine". It is often said that this or that much of the variance in IQ is "determined" by heredity. What is determined is not the actual intellectual performances of a given person but the *range of possible reactions* he might display (e.g. in a test) given the opportunity to act under specified circumstances. The behaviours, from which a certain personality trait is inferred, are conditioned by the interplay between genes and emerging situations. "Heredity is not a status but a process. Genetic traits are not preformed in the sex cells, but emerge in the course of development..." (*op. cit.*, p. 4).

It has often been maintained that the measured average differences that are consistently found between lower and upper class children in both IQ and scholastic attainments are largely accounted for by the "genetic stratification" taking place in an open society with a certain amount of social mobility. Dobzhansky refers to the experience derived from caste systems, for instance in India, where after thousands of years of genetic isolation and inbreeding the lower castes come up with young people who succeed in school as well as do those of upper caste origin. From a genetic point of view this should not be surprising, because the human species, like other outbreeding species, has an "enormous store of variability. Even with artificial selection directioned specifically towards this end, it is practically impossible to obtain a population completely homozygous for all its genes" (*op. cit.*, p. 32). A caste or a rigid social class system leads to a wastage of talent, since those who are talented are impeded from getting the education or entering the occupations for which their abilities qualify them. By systematically admitting to further education those whose more or less inherited capacities qualify them for it, the society enhances the importance of biological inheritance for success.

Equality between various social, racial, and ethnic groups has often been confused with *equal representation*. A substantial portion of the survey research relevant to the problem of "reserve of talent" pertains to the representation that various social classes have in, for instance, upper secondary schools and at universities (Husén, 1972). The tremendous differences found in these surveys provided ample justification to hypothesize that a large proportion of talented young people of lower class background did not get the opportunity to enter further education and therefore belonged to the "ability reserve". But imbalances of this size aside, one cannot jump to the conclusion that any imbalance, however small it may be, is due to "inequality of opportunity". Dobzhansky points out that a model of full representational equality between various social and other groups implies that *all* the personality traits needed for scholastic success are only environmentally conditioned and randomly distributed over social strata.

Even if we assume that genetically determined intelligence has the same distribution in all strata we still have to consider other factors which account for some fifty per cent of the differences in scholastic achievement and which by massive research have been shown to be conditioned by home background, including such factors as parental education, verbal environment, and attitude toward school and learning (Vernon, 1950). Individuals vary not only in their intellectual capacity but also in their capacity to take advantage of the opportunities that are offered them. Both these capacities can be assumed to be in part genetically conditioned.

Equality of opportunity has two main aspects. In the first place, according to the classical conception, everybody, regardless of social origin, is entitled to have access to the various tracks which, not least through the formal educational systems, lead to various social positions and economic levels. Thus, everybody should have the right to strive and compete. Secondly, equality should also be conceived of as the right to be treated differently according to one's particular assets. Different inherited capacities require different environments if they are to develop to the satisfaction of the individual. Dobzhansky (1973) points out that a potential musical virtuoso should not be barred from entering a conservatory by being channeled into a training program for engineers. "Ideal equality would entail provision of a set of diverse educational paths which people will choose ... in accord with their tastes and abilities" (*op. cit.*, pp. 41–2).

IMCOMPATIBILITIES AND DILEMMAS

Heckhausen (1973), a leading researcher in the field of motivation, has made an attempt to analyze the meaning of equality of opportunity (*Chancengleichheit*) in the context of achievement-motivated behavior. He thereby distinguishes between two kinds of such behavior, the work-oriented and the excellence-oriented. The first has to do with whether the individual sees himself as trying hard or not, and refers to an essentially subjective evaluation. The second is related to norms of reference that are social, the evaluation of one's performance by the group – the school, the work group, the organization, and the society at large.

Heckhausen points out that the conception of formal equality of opportunity views performance according to rules similar to the ones in sport. The policy implications are that equal external conditions at a given occasion for competitive performance should be established. The focus is on the common *starting line* for all the runners and not on the line marking the goal for the run. The perspective is a cross-sectional one, which limits the problem to the one of equality of opportunity to *demonstrate* actual capacity. But in a longitudinal perspective the question becomes one of what degree of equality there is for the individual to *develop* his potential capacity.

An increasing amount of evidence suggests that the imbalances between various social strata among students of comparable IQ in participation in higher or advanced education are not to be attributed primarily to differences of a material or economic character but to psychological factors operating differently in various strata, such as aspiration for further education, parental support, information about educational possibilities, etc. Many of these factors could be subsumed under the heading "motivation for mobility".

The problem of bringing about increased equality is beset with various dilemmas which should, as Heckhausen points out, be made explicit and not swept under the rug. A clarification of these dilemmas can be very helpful for the policy makers and lay the basis for more realistic social and educational policy.

The first basic dilemma or incompatibility is that the school has to serve a principle counteracting equality in attainments. The school is there to impart competence and therefore emphasizes individual achievements which are evaluated according to a common scale. These normative evaluations form the basis for progressive selection and differentiation as the individual moves up the educational ladder. Differing amounts of ability and motivation progressively create increased individual differences in cognitive competence.

A second dilemma is that equality of opportunity requires not equal but different offerings. When initial differences in any important respect already exist between pupils, uniform offerings or treatments often cannot but increase these differences. A cumulative learning deficit develops under such circumstances among the initially retarded. Equality of support is consistently promoted when compensatory treatment is provided to those who initially are lagging behind.

A third dilemma emerges if the second one is resolved according to what is implied by different and not uniform offerings, i.e., radical individualization. A differentiation of offerings according to individual optimal capacities can easily increase the differences among those who are the recipients. Only by applying what Heckhausen calls the "inverted principle of performance", that is by providing more learning time and other compensatory devices, can the consequences of individualized initial offerings to some extent be counteracted.

Integrated and differentiated school system in different ways can promote equality of opportunity. An integrated, comprehensive system is to the advantage of pupils who are underprivileged with regard to educational and social background. Thus, the study of equality of educational opportunity by Coleman (1966) and his associates suggested strongly that the underprivileged Black pupils profited more by going to integrated than to segregated schools. But integration mainly promotes equality in terms of leveling out *initial* differences in opportunity (*Chancenausgleich*). At the same time it does not always promote the intellectual development of the most able pupils who thus may be hampered by the slowness of progress of their less able classmates. These pupils are therefore in a way not having equal opportunity for an optimal development. Whether and to what extent this is the case is still an open question chiefly because it is a matter of interpretation on the basis of value judgments.

The evaluation of pupil achievements is as a rule *normative*, that is to say, their achievements are compared with each other's and therefore related to some kind of norm or standard, whether they are simply ranked or are inserted on a percentile or standard scale. The outcome of such a normative evaluation of the individual pupil progressively determines his further career in education. Normative evaluation is part and parcel of a competitive system, wherein selection and progressive differentiation are the main features.

A *criterion-referenced evaluation*, in contrast, aims at setting objectives for the learning process which under normal circumstances can be achieved by the majority of the pupils (Bloom *et al.*, 1971). Initial failure to reach the goal would then be primarily regarded not as a defect inherent in the pupil, for which he is held back, but as a defect in the teaching process, such as having devoted too little time or chosen the wrong media in presenting the learning material to him. All the criteria together define a basic level or common course (*Sockelniveau*) which practically all the students could be expected to reach. The problem of setting the appropriate level is of course a dilemma: the higher it is set the more disparity in the end results. The requirements embodied in the set of objectives that make up the basic level depend heavily upon the societal setting. As has been amply brought out in the International Study of Educational Achievements (IEA), there are tremendous differences between the industrialized and the non-industrialized countries in terms of average achievements in the various school subjects (Comber and Keeves, 1973; Thorndike, 1973). These differences depend only to a minor extent on the quality of the teaching offered, and are simply reflections of the general social and educational background of the pupils. In their reading comprehension scores, those who come from illiterate backgrounds are still after several years of formal schooling one to two standard deviations below those whose parents are literate.

A problem which several authors have brought up (e.g. Bell, 1973 and Dobzhansky, 1973) and which has been discussed at several places in this book has to do with values attached to various types of human performance. In the industrial – and perhaps even more so in the post-industrial – society, certain cognitive skills, particularly as they are certified by the school, tend to determine social status. But the association also works the other way around: Social status tends to determine the development of cognitive skills. Heckhausen points out: "The more developed the school system in a society is, the more it tries to ascertain equality of opportunity for all, the more mandatory schooling is extended in time and the more ambitious the learning goals, the more differentiated the marking system becomes, the more allocation to various occupational positions is made on the basis of performances and not on ascriptive status criteria, then the more active is the upward and downward mobility over borderlines between strata from generation to generation, the more the growing generation will become selected according to its aptitudes and levels of performance, in spite of the imperfections of such a procedure in individual cases".

Opportunity for further education does not necessarily provide an extended repertoire of future options. Further education even though it might be of a general character, as is often the case with the basic university degree, means that certain other furthergoing types of education are eliminated from the repertoire of options. Education at an advanced level becomes progressively specialized and narrow in comparison to the whole "menu" available at earlier stages. Up to the end of mandatory schooling the curriculum is, as far as its intellectual content is concerned, rather balanced in terms of presenting the humanities, science, mathematics, and the social sciences in such proportions as are supposed to prepare the citizen for the society he is going to live in. In the academic secondary school which is preparatory for higher education he often has to specialize in one area, although the others are not entirely neglected. But when he enters the university further specialization is required within the area of his previous specialization.

Finally, it is appropriate to ask the seldom-raised question: "Opportunity for what?" It is generally taken as self-evident that the more formal education that is successfully completed, the more opportunity in terms of various career paths is opened up. It is true that the more formal education a person has, the higher in terms of status are the occupations opened up to him and the higher his earnings. The occupations that become accessible are seen as more difficult and complex in terms of requirements and recruitment to them is surrounded by a system of credentials and legitimizing rules of admission. What is meant when one speaks of equalizing opportunities is the vertical climbing within socially established hierarchies of status, prestige and income. Very often overlooked is the *horizontal* diversity of opportunities or options reflecting a broad spectrum of interests, needs and aptitudes which are only weakly correlated with scholastic ability. Such options need to become operationalized.

The analysis of the dilemmas which have to be faced in attempts to bring about more equality of educational opportunity leads Heckhausen (1973) to seven major policy guidelines which in his view are instrumental to implementing the goals of such a policy. He emphasizes, however, that they are conducive primarily to the leveling out rather than to actively bringing about more equality.

The guidelines are:

(1) A "multiversity" of pre-school education related to the life around the child,
(2) social integration and individualization within a comprehensive school,
(3) criterion-referenced evaluation in allocation of further chances on the basis of the "inverted principle of achievement",
(4) an ambitious level of common competence (*Sockelniveau*) for all pupils,
(5) horizontal extension of chances as opposed to vertical loss of chances,
(6) recurrent education, and
(7) revision of the system of credentials and *Laufbahn*.

IS MODERN SOCIETY BECOMING INCREASINGLY MERITOCRATIC?

As has been pointed out earlier, at the core of the classical liberal conception of equality has been the idea that careers should be open to talent, and once they have been opened, the competition to "struggle ahead" should be fair. Thus, those who possess genuine talent – and, of course, the desire to "use" it – deserve to be supported. This was, for instance, the idea behind the free places for poor boys in the grammar school in England and the stipends available for pupils from lower class homes who would otherwise not have the opportunity to obtain the advanced education their talent qualified them for. The liberal idea of opening careers to the talented has been fittingly referred to by Frankel (1973) as "corrective egalitarianism". It is built on two tacit assumptions. In the first place, by putting everybody on the scratch line, all would have a fair chance, i.e., the same opportunity, to show their worth in the ensuing race. Those who quit the race or fell behind had only themselves to blame. They had been given the chance, and their talent and/or motivation apparently did not suffice. Secondly, by having everybody start from the same baseline, i.e., by giving them a certain number of years of common schooling, nobody was, at least at that point, given any undue advantage or any unjust handicap.

Both these assumptions have been challenged. Firstly, to start from scratch, that is to say, to spend a certain number of years of regular schooling together, is a purely formal kind of equality. What happens to a child during his pre-school years, before he enters the formal educational system, is of decisive importance for his ability to compete later on. Secondly, what happens to the pupils once they have entered school is closely related to their social background. A considerable survey research has shown that dropout rate and grade-repeating vary considerably between social strata (Husén and Boalt, 1968). The failure rate for grammar school pupils in England who according to the eleven-plus examination belonged to the best third of the intake was 10 per cent among pupils with professional and managerial background as compared to 38 and 54 per cent for those whose fathers were semi-skilled and unskilled workers respectively (HMSO, 1954).

Under the impact of the enthusiasm prevailing at the beginning of the 1960's, when education was regarded as the major booster of economic growth, it was hoped that changes in the structure of educational system could bring about broadened, more equitable participation in advanced education. However, the background papers prepared for the OECD Policy Conference on Educational Growth in 1970 cited surveys which showed that in spite of massive expansion of enrollment the imbalances in participation with regard to social class, sex and ethnicity were very much the same as they had been some ten years earlier (OECD, 1970). There were large differences in results between social classes, sexes and ethnic groups. These disappointing findings gave rise to soul-searching basic questions. Is formal equality of opportunity not enough? Do we have to make provisions for greater equality of outcomes, for instance in seeing to it that greater opportunities of "acquiring intelligence" are provided?

But a different question also had to be posed. Is the meritocratic element a necessary corollary of the modern, highly industrialized society, not to speak of the post-industrial society that is emerging above the horizon? This second problem can be formulated as follows: Is the meritocratic orientation with its emphasis on cognitive competence irresistibly leading to a society where educated intelligence becomes even more important as a social stratifier? We shall deal with this more closely in the latter part of this chapter.

On his large canvas, *The Coming of Post-Industrial Society*, Daniel Bell (1973) tries to depict the role of the "technocrats" in this type of society. What he says about them can be regarded as a preamble to the section in his "Coda" on "Meritocracy and Equality". The paradigm employed in his analysis is the movement of mankind toward greater rationality, of which industrialization is one expression. What he envisages for the post-industrial society is the "new centrality of *theoretical* knowledge, the primacy of theory over empiricism, and the codification of knowledge into abstract systems of symbols that can be translated into many different and varied circumstances. Every society now lives by innovation and growth, and it is theoretical knowledge that has become the matrix of innovation" (*op. cit.*, pp. 343 *et seq.*). This means, then, that instead of property and political criteria the basis of power will in the future progressively become knowledge proper. The dominant figures will no longer be the entrepreneurs, the businessmen, the industrial executives but the "scientists, the mathematicians, the economists, and the engineers of the new technology" (p. 344). "The husbanding of talent and the spread of educational and intellectual institutions will become a prime concern of the society; not only the best talents but eventually the entire complex of prestige and status will be rooted in the intellectual and scientific communities" (p. 344). This clearly means that the technocrats, those who exercise authority by virtue of technical competence, will become the influential people. "In the post-industrial society, technical skill becomes the base of and education the mode of access to power; those (or the elite of the group) who come to the fore in this fashion are the scientists" (p. 358). "The rise of the new elites based on skills derives from the simple fact that knowledge and planning ... have become the basic requisites for all organized action in a modern society" (p. 362). The importance of technical competence as a source of influence is further enhanced by the fact that property as a basis of power is weakened. In the first place it has increasingly become corporate and controlled by managers, private or public. Secondly, property has increasingly become invisible: It consists more and more of rights or obligations, such as right to education, to welfare, to pension, etc.

Bell's proposition of an inherent and growing element of meritocracy replacing property in determining social stratification in the post-industrial society has been challenged by representatives of Marxist-oriented social philosophies. Bell sees factors determining a growing meritocracy, such as new technologies, bureaucratic control and expanding knowledge production, prevail in both capitalist and socialist countries. Lasch (1973) in reviewing Bell's book refutes the conception of a "new class" of meritocrats. Those who could be subsumed under this category have certain common characteristics but lack what would constitute them as a "class", i.e., common interests. The ability to initiate ideas does not necessarily lead to power. The experts and researchers tend increasingly to be supported by public money, which means that the power emanating from the utilization of expertise tend to accrue to the State on which the experts become more and more dependent.

MERITOCRACY AND EQUALITY

Modern society is beset with a basic dilemma, which has so provocatively been spelled out by Michael Young in his fable *The Rise of the Meritocracy* (1958). On the one hand it seeks to implement the principle of equality of opportunity: Everybody should have full access to education within the limits of his talent. On the other hand, a systematic implementation of such a policy could in the long run lead to a society with a hereditary meritocracy, because irrespective of the degree of "purification" of the gene pool one could expect the parents who initially "made it" into the meritocracy to pass on their social (and genetic) advantages to their children.

In a society based on competition, which is considered to be indispensable for motivating people, such a dilemma is bound to prevail. It is not basically resolved by a socialist system of production (Feldmesser, 1957; Sauvy *et al.*, 1973). It is apparent that in the Soviet Union a meritocracy of scientists, engineers, party bureaucrats and intellectuals of the arts has emerged and is with regard to both prestige and remuneration a privileged group. It is also obvious that this group, which has developed over more than half a century, has been able to pass on its privileges to the next generation, not in terms of material wealth but of educated and status-conscious home background. When Premier Krushchev introduced the new Education Act to the Supreme Soviet in 1958 he pointed out that the majority of students at institutions of higher learning came from homes of the "intelligentsia and the functionaries", while those whose parents were workers and peasants, that is the majority of the people, represented the minority (Sauvy *et al.*, 1973, p. 28). What has later been reported both from the Soviet Union and from Poland (Szczepanski, 1963, Yanowitch and Dodge, 1968) has confirmed the enrollment picture as being dominated by students from professional and managerial backgrounds.

Janina Lagneau in her study of access to higher education in the socialist countries points out that the majority of the intelligentsia in countries like the Soviet Union and Poland is "first-generation intelligentsia" whose parents were workers or peasants. Because of the imbalances between the social categories among the university students regulations have been issued which in fact give certain credits to those who come from less privileged homes in competing for places at the university. Such regulations are perceived by those of privileged background to penalize them. Those who according to the official rhetoric have "contributed the most to the advancement of the underprivileged classes, and were given the task of forming the core of a socialist intelligentsia, find themselves paradoxically downgraded in the sense that their children are penalized when taking entrance examinations in comparison with the children of parents who have remained workers and peasants" (Sauvy *et al.*, p. 49; cf. Lipset, 1972). Lagneau sees tendencies among those who "made it" to the intelligentsia to stand out as a "new middle class, jealous of its only privilege which is that of higher education" (Sauvy *et al.*, *ibid.*).

There is also another dilemma. Lagneau (Sauvy *et al.*, 1973 p. 25) points out that in the socialist countries the "primary and ideological concern has been to rapidly improve the education of the previously underprivileged classes – working class and peasant class – but this aim very quickly came into conflict with the immediate aim of the economic structure for managers and technicians".

If the meritocracy-equality dilemma seems to beset both capitalist and socialist economies, how then is it going to be resolved in the future? Bell maintains that the post-industrial society "in its initial logic" is a meritocracy. On the other hand, Marxist social scientists contend, as we have seen earlier, that the "meritocratic legitimation mechanisms", such as credentials, school marks and test scores, are instruments by means of which the ruling class tries to keep workers in line, i.e., to dominate them. In order to prove that this is the case the proponents of this view would be compelled to show that formal schooling and assessed cognitive skills per se do not play any decisive role in building occupational competence or promoting the national economy, and that what really counts is social class. One basic problem, then, in attempting to resolve the dilemma becomes that of finding out to what extent educated intelligence and technical skill now and in the future can be regarded as assets both for the individual and for the society. There is overwhelming evidence advanced by economists and educational sociologists that both the individual and society benefit from education. These benefits may be of various kinds, material and psychological. They comprise earnings, status, influence, and power. It is another matter that the role of schooling has been exaggerated by confounding its "effect" with those of social background and potential or inherited intelligence. The present author has presented longitudinal data on the predictive power of social background, formal schooling and early IQ which show that discounting for social background substantially reduces the correlation between education and adult earnings. But it by no means reduces it to an insignificant level (Husén, 1969).

The other basic problem has to do with the influence of the inherited or potential IQ. Those who take the view that the heritability of individual IQ is high, i.e., that on the average individual differences in intellectual performance within a given population are accounted for mainly by genetic factors, as a matter of consequence take the view that the number of persons with high IQ represents a strictly limited pool of talent. If this is the case, the objective for a liberal policy of establishing equality of educational opportunity should be to see to it that those individuals, irrespective of their social and geographical origin, are brought to the top in the social hierarchy, where they "belong". They are the "natural aristocracy" that Jefferson once talked about as opposed to the ascriptive nobility.

The problem of IQ and meritocracy has been brought out in a rather provocative way by Richard Herrnstein of Harvard University. On the assumption that studies of identical twins brought up apart and together had shown that heredity accounted for 80 per cent of the differences in IQ, he brought out the consequences in the form of a syllogism (Herrnstein, 1971):

"1. If differences in mental abilities are inherited, and
2. if success requires those abilities, and
3. if earnings and prestige depend on success,
4. then social standing will be based to some extent on inherited differences among people.

True?   False?"

He arrives at the conclusion that observed social class differences in intellectual achievement and success are "to some extent" dependent upon inherited differences. It would be fair to say that the majority of the researchers who have dealt empirically with these problems would go along with Herrnstein in attributing *some* influence to hereditary factors.

Herrnstein's overall conclusion has certain corollaries which he spells out in his 1971 article and develops further in his book *IQ in the Meritocracy* (1973). In the first place, the heritability of IQ will rise. Secondly, social mobility will progressively become more closely related to innate intelligence. Thirdly, very able people will accumulate at the top of the social pyramid. Fourthly, low IQ individuals will amass at the bottom. Fifthly, low IQ individuals will by heredity become an unemployed proletariat. Attempts to implement a radical, "redemptive" egalitarianism could easily result in a society wherein hereditary assets play a much more important role so as to create a social stratification that is essentially a "virtual caste system". Therefore, the present class society with mobility to cross class boundaries via the route of its competitive reward system is to be preferred. "The opportunity for social mobility across classes assures the biological distinctiveness of each class, for the unusual offspring ... would quickly rise above his family or sink below it, and take his place, both biologically, with his peers. The traffic is significant these days, for the lower classes produce, in sheer numbers, more people with high IQ's than the upper classes ... simply because they are so large a proportion of the total population" (Herrnstein, 1973, p. 220).

A radical policy of egalitarianism of results would diminish the size of the lower class, raise heritability, widen the "ability gap" between classes, and create a caste system wherein there would be no traffic across class boundaries. The classes would become increasingly alienated from each other. The liberal, "corrective" egalitarianism accepts a class society wherein social status is achieved in a "fair" way but prevents the creation of a hereditary aristocracy. "By removing arbitrary barriers between classes, society achieves the laudable goal of allowing people of different races, religions, and ethnic backgrounds to earn any level of status, but, simultaneously, it fosters biological barriers to mobility. When people can freely take their natural level in society, the upper classes will, virtually by definition, have greater capacity than the lower" (*op. cit.*, p. 221).

Herrnstein, to be sure, is right in saying that "by definition" upper class is at the top and lower class is at the bottom of the status scale. Within the framework of his value premises the logic behind Herrnstein's reasoning would seem to be the following:

1) There is an objective set of traits lumped together under the label "intelligence" (IQ);
2) Individual and groups differences in intelligence have a large genetic component;
3) Intelligence is valuable for many high-level jobs in society of today;
4) Therefore, differences in IQ play an important role in accounting for differences in occupational success and social status.

But he does not bring out the value premises upon which his logic rests. The key words in the last sentence in the quotation above are "natural level" and "capacity". On the basis of what values are the criteria of stratification arrived at? In an attempt to analyze the concept of talent the present author arrived at the conclusion that the issue whether upper-class pupils are more "intelligent" than lower-class pupils is a pseudoproblem, "because the answer could logically be derived from the way the problem is posed" (Husén, 1972). The tests employed have been validated against criteria of success in our type of society, such as the ability to succeed in school or in the occupation hierarchy. This is to say, the criteria are based on certain dominant values in our society, values that, in a way, determine its "power structure". "If we keep in mind that intelligence is defined by the dominant socio-cultural reference system, and that in the value structure guiding the system over-riding priority has been attached to the ability to succeed in scholastic pursuits, one should not be surprised to find that upperclass students have higher IQ's than lower-class students and that Whites perform better than Blacks" (Husén, 1972, pp. 55–56).

In an article on "IQ, Social Class and Educational Policy" Eysenck (1973) makes a case for genetic social class differences of tested intelligence. He cites studies on twins who are brought up apart and on similarities between foster children and their adoption parents as compared to their biological parents, and regards the proportion 80 per cent genetic factors and 20 per cent environmental factors in accounting for observed variance in IQ as firmly proven. But the strongest argument in favor of the decisive influence of genetic factors on ability he finds in the well-known phenomenon of regression toward the mean, which was first studied by Galton. In a diagram he illustrates how children's IQ's regress on father's IQ so that those from professional families with fathers having an average IQ of 140 are found to have an IQ of 120 and children of workers with an IQ of 90 themselves get an average of 100. He quotes from a study conducted by Cyril Burt on intergeneration change of social status. Only about half of those whose fathers were in the upper or upper middle class ended up in the same status category as their parents. The same applied to those of working class background, only some 50 per cent remaining in their original category. The rest moved up the social status ladder with 14 per cent reaching the top. A considerable degree of social mobility could similarly be observed in a follow-up study from 1938 to 1964 of some 700 males (Husén, 1969, pp. 164 *et seq.*), whose social status according to the Roe (1962) six-point scale at the age of 35 was compared with that of the father 26 years earlier. About 50 per cent of those with professional and managerial background had moved to a lower status, 18 per cent being in the working class categories. About one fifth of those with working class background had moved to sub-professional or professional-managerial positions. Thus, in a way, the regression mechanism can be regarded as a hereditary guarantee of social mobility: "... the bright rise, the dull sink on the social scale" (Eysenck, *op. cit.*, p. 80).

The "statistically inevitable" social mobility that Eysenck infers from the regression effect and the constant spread in IQ between generations (which he evidently regards as proven) seems, however, to be beset with certain snags. For instance, a comparison between generations in terms of occupational status is strongly affected by the far-reaching restructuring of the labor market which is part of the change to a post-industrial, service economy. The proportion of manual jobs has decreased, and the white-collar ones have increased. In the Malmö follow-up study white-collar jobs had increased from 20 to about 40 per cent from 1938 to 1964.

REDEFINITION OF EQUALITY AND MERITOCRACY

As has been pointed out in another context, one can discern three conceptions of equality in education (Husén, 1972). The conservative conception is that of a metaphysically ascriptive society, wherein each individual is born to the conditions that God has determined for him. The liberal conception envisages a formally open society wherein the individual is prime mover, and should be free to move ahead and to realize his potentialities as much as he desires. Once external barriers of economic and geographical character have been removed it is up to the individual to get into the competition and prove himself. If he has the "ability" and "will" to go ahead he certainly is earmarked for success. If his ability or his will does not suffice he has nobody but himself to blame. Once the school system treats everybody equally in terms of giving them access and the needed resources of instruction, the school can serve as a "great equalizer" and a powerful agent for change in our society. The trouble is, as has been noted earlier, the two objectives – providing everybody with formal equality of opportunity to enter the race and achieving greater social and economic equality – are far from compatible. The liberal type of equality means that everybody is given the opportunity to run the competitive race according to his ability and motivation. The formal school system is a system of credentials that progressively establishes, reinforces and legitimizes *distinctions* in adult careers.

The evident failure to bring about greater equality in turn gave rise to a debate in which a distinction was drawn between equality of opportunity and equality of outcomes, the latter providing a third conception of equality. Frankel (1973) speaks of a "corrective" and a "redemptive" egalitarianism. The latter equality has been defined by Coleman (1968) as equality in acquiring the intelligence or the skills needed to absorb the knowledge imparted by the formal school system. The demand for the "open university" and for "fair representation" of students in institutions of higher learning from various racial, ethnic and social class categories is another reflection of the conception of equality of outcomes or results (Karabel, 1973). Evidently, if one wants to maintain certain standards of access and/or of results, neither completely open access nor complete equality of results can be achieved as long as those entering the system differ in terms of social background and genetically conditioned ability. In *all* the countries participating in the so-called Six-Subject Survey conducted by the International Association for the Evaluation of Educational Achievement, irrespective of whether they were socialist or capitalist, industrial or agricultural, the home background (including both "native wit" and environment) accounted for more of the between-school and between-student differences in achievement than all the school and instructional factors together. This implies, then, that equality of outcomes, provided that school achievements are only to a modest extent reflections of genetic differences, cannot be brought about unless an almost uniform society in terms of economic conditions is established. But not even that would suffice, because initial differences among the various kinds of psychological atmosphere in which children are nurtured would have to be leveled out, which could in theory only be done by establishing some system of institutions whereby greater uniformity in child-rearing could be guaranteed.

Bell (1973) points out that equality of results can only be achieved in a communal-socialist society. As a main object of social policy "it will demand an entirely new political agenda for the social systems of advanced industrial countries" (*op. cit.*, p. 433). The agenda cannot succeed unless it is rooted in a "new ethic", a completely new conception of fairness. This new socialist ethic is based upon the assumption that it will be possible to bring about allegiance not by material but by philosophical rewards.

To be sure, the post-industrial society that Bell himself envisages is not based upon the assumption of the prevalence of a consistent communal ethic in the decades to come but upon the meritocratic assumption that educated ability will become the basis of power and influence as well as of economic growth. But does this mean that we can expect individual competition in the arena of formal schooling and research to become even more rugged, since success in life will very much depend on the extent to which a person succeeds in realizing his potentialities in terms of marketable skills and coping behavior in his habitat?

This question leads us to take a closer look at both equality and meritocracy as concepts. Bell (1973) points out that equality in terms of universalism, equality before the law, universal access to some schooling and other basic social services does not imply equality all along the line. What, then, could be conceived of as "a just meritocracy" or, to put it the other way around, "a just equality"?

The confusion that has been created in the debate about equality stems largely from the fact that use of a common label is conducive to the conception that we have to do with a unitary and well-defined entity whereas the word refers to many aspects of human affairs. Equality can be regarded as describing a psychological fact. Individuals or groups of individuals may be aware that human conditions vary but they may or may not perceive these conditions, which can be material and/or status differences, as just or unjust. The stratification in terms of power, influence and/or remuneration that always exists in a society, independent of its basic economic system, may or may not be perceived as "unequal" and therefore perhaps as unjust. The point is that there are many dimensions (psychological and subjective as well as material and objective) of inequality, which are not necessarily positively correlated with each other. For example, within certain occupational categories earnings are negatively correlated with amount of leisure time, i.e., those who work more tend to have a larger income, particularly in cases where they are paid on a piece-rate basis.

Bell points out that certain objectives of a "rigid, ideological egalitarianism" could come in conflict with other social objectives, such as rational use of competence, a conflict that has also been pointed out by Lagneau (Sauvy *et al.*, 1973). A still more serious conflict is the one that can occur when equality in rewards is extended to groups or categories so that they are distributed according to quotas, regardless of qualifications.

If a highly competent person were not paid more than one less competent in the same field there would be a tendency among those who for instance are seeking service to go to the more competent in matters that could easily be handled by the less competent. Thus, one can arrive at a rational basis for inequality in, say, remuneration by tying it to certain competencies as assessed by experts in the field. A rationale for the kind of "just" meritocracy that Bell envisages in the post-industrial society is the classical distinction between power and authority. Power is entitlement to command, in the last resort backed up by overt force. "Authority is a competence based upon skill, learning, talent, artistry or some similar attribute" (*op. cit.*, p. 453). He therefore arrives at the definition of a meritocracy as "those who have earned their authority" (*ibid.*). This earned status is something the individual has had bestowed on him by his peers. "The meritocracy, in the best meaning of that word, is made up of those worthy of praise. They are the men who are the best in their fields, as judged by their fellows" (p. 454).

It is indeed, as has been intimated above, difficult to conceive of an egalitarian society wherein the material differences would be reduced to an insignificant level. A communal society of that type would have to return to a pattern of production of both goods and services that would be far below the present level. Needless to say, it would be entirely incompatible with the basic assumptions upon which the post-industrial society is envisioned. Both the system of production and the "planning system" (Galbraith, 1973) would have to become markedly meritocratic in terms of drawing upon genuine competence in order to solve increasingly more complicated problems. The hierarchical order would become more pronounced than at present both in public administration and in public and private enterprise. This, in turn, implies that the authority is to be bestowed upon those who have the competence to use it. The political process then becomes even more beset with the problem of "grass-root participation", which perhaps in the long run is a problem of communication between those who are elected to exercise power and authority and their followers.

Over and above certain basic equalities, such as equality before the law, equal access to certain public services, and the right to be regarded and treated equally as human beings, the equality problem in the post-industrial society can be expected to be one of *communication* between the "meritocratic complex" and the rest of the citizens. This is at the core of the "participation" problem which in recent years has increasingly become acute in the highly industrialized and bureaucratized societies.

In accord with the more functional and in its value premises more liberal conception of social development are we heading toward a more integrated society with expanded basic equality and less segregation? Increased affluence should be conducive to the solution of problems and tensions pertaining to social class, race and ethnicity. Or in accord with the socialist-Marxist conception of polarization, is society becoming increasingly more dominated by a growing monopolistic capitalism with increased inequalities and growing tensions until a revolutionary situation completely rearranges the social order?

The integration and polarization theories can be regarded as extremes on a continuum: the actual societal development, depending upon the value-preferences in the decades up to the year 2000, will be characterized by a pattern somewhere in between. Jensen *et al.* (1973) in their projection of alternative futures for European education have spelled out three. Their first model is essentially a reflection of the liberal conception of society and envisages a future in which the educational system increasingly will serve a growing economy, while the third one emphasizes the socialization function of the school. The second model reflects the values of a "mixed economy". Here the educational system is expected to prepare the individual for serving the economy but at the same time to provide greater equality of opportunity by promoting his self-realization in a flexible formal school structure which does not necessarily prepare him for a particular slot. It is this model which has by and large served as a guideline for educational change in Sweden, as well as in other countries with similar social and economic orientations.

In modern highly industrialized society the answer to the question how much of meritocracy we are heading for is evidently closely related to the valuation of economic growth and to what constitutes or is detrimental to "progress", the "good life" or the "quality of life". As long as educated intelligence is conceived of mainly as an investment in economic growth, those who have achieved merit in this respect will tend to be singled out for special reward, that is, to be better paid and to be elevated to power and influence.

The question then arises whether a "zero-growth" philosophy in the society will do away with meritocracy in terms of letting rewards accrue to those who are more "intelligent", more "skillful", or have acquired more "merits". Even under "zero-growth" conditions a complex society and its economic machinery has to be kept running. Sufficient numbers of people with the skills needed to manufacture goods, render services, coordinate and administer activities at different levels have to be trained. The mere fact that we find meritocratic tendencies prevailing in both capitalist and socialist economies leads us to conclude that these tendencies are inherent in the highly industrialized society itself.

CHAPTER 7

STANDARD OF THE ELITE IN SELECTIVE AND COMPREHENSIVE SYSTEMS

TWO TYPES OF SCHOOL STRUCTURE — TWO EDUCATIONAL PHILOSOPHIES

The "enrollment explosion" at the secondary school level and the expanded admission to the university-preparing school as well as to the university itself has given rise to questions about the "standard" of the students processed through a system of mass education as compared to an élitist one. The present author has dealt with the problem of comprehensiveness versus élitism in other connections (Husén, 1962 and 1973). Suffice it to indicate here that the criteria of "standards" are not as self-evident as they might seem *prima facie,* simply because the comprehensive system is based on partly other values than the élitist and therefore cannot be evaluated according to identical criteria. The very term "standard" has had a time-honoured place in educational folklore. The danger of "lowered standards" has often been pointed out by those who oppose broadening access to advanced education.

One of the problems singled out for particular analysis in the survey research conducted by the International Association for the Evaluation of Educational Achievement (IEA) has for a long time been a central policy issue in Europe, namely whether and the extent to which a comprehensive school system should replace the prevailing selective one. The IEA Project provided an unprecedented opportunity to compare what happens to the superior students when upper secondary school enrollment is broadened. The reason for the passion that often has gone into the debate on the comprehensive versus the selective school is that it is not merely didactic principles or methods of organizing the curriculum that are at issue. At the heart of the matter we find two opposing educational philosophies reflecting strong vested interests. On one hand we have the egalitarian and reconstructivist view, and on the other, the by and large conservative and élitist view of the educational system.

A comprehensive system provides a publicly supported school education for all children of mandatory school age in a given catchment area. This means that all programs or curricular offerings are provided in the same school unit. Another essential feature of comprehensiveness is that no differentiation or grouping practices that definitively determine the ensuing educational and occupational careers are employed. Children from all walks of life are taken care of.

In a selective system children are by means of organizational differentiation at an early age allocated to different types of school, and, also at an early stage of their school career, grouping practices are employed aiming at spotting those who are supposed to be particularly academically-oriented. Apart from selective admission and grouping, the system is as a rule also characterized by a high attrition rate in terms of grade-repeating and drop-out.

In the debate on the relative merits and drawbacks of the two systems it has been maintained, on the one hand, that the top pupils in a comprehensive system will suffer by having to be taught together with their more slow-learning peers. This will impair their standard of achievement in comparison with pupils of equal intellectual standing in systems where an organizational differentiation in terms of selection for separate academically oriented schools takes place at an early age or where strict homogeneous grouping within the school is employed.

The adherents of comprehensive education, on the other hand, maintain that the top pupils will not suffer as much in their system as the great mass of the less academically-oriented students in a selective system, particularly those who rather early are left in the elementary school after the "book-oriented" have been selected for the university-preparing secondary schools.

The élitists maintain that a system of selection based on fair and equally employed criteria of excellence will open the avenues to high-status occupation to those from all walks of life who deserve it by possessing the necessary (mainly inherited) talent. The comprehensivists counter by claiming that a selective system is beset with a greater social bias than the comprehensive one. As one moves up the ladder of the formal educational system the proportion of lower-class pupils is much lower in a selective than in a comprehensive system, which is interpreted as evidence for bias.

The two propositions, both the one on the standard of the élite and the one on social bias, were tested on national systems of education in the first two large-scale surveys conducted by IEA (Husén, 1967; Postlethwaite, 1967; Comber and Keeves, 1973). The national systems of education differ tremendously with regard to the size of the pre-university group (in per cent of the relevant age groups). In the mathematics study this group varied from less than 10 per cent in some European countries to more than 70 per cent in the United States. In the Science study (stage 2) the variation was by and large of the same order of magnitude. The variability in Europe had, how-ever, decreased somewhat. Evidently, there is no point in making comparisons between mean performances behind which there are school populations representing such variations in terms of the pro-portion of the relevant age group. Thus, it was decided to take advan-tage of the IEA survey data for Population 4, that is to say, pupils who are in the terminal grade of the pre-university school. Typical national illustrations of this population are for instance the *Oberprimaner* in Germany, the pupils who are about to sit for the GCE A-level in England, and for the *baccalauréat* in France.

The problem of "comparing" the terminal pupils is not as simple as it might appear from the popular debate on the relative "standard" of secondary systems with a rather strict selection versus those with an open door policy. The problem of whether the one or the other system is to be preferred is a matter of what criteria one wants to employ in evaluating them, and therefore in the last run a question of political preferences. Even if the evaluators can agree upon what criteria should be employed, they will certainly put them in different orders of prior-ity. The adherent of an élitist system tends to evaluate the schools in terms of the quality of their *end-products*, either leaving out those who are lost in the selection and/or attrition process or attaching a lower priority to their educational fate. The comprehensivist prefers to look at what happens to the great mass of students. His overriding question is: How many are brought how far?

STANDARD OF THE ELITE IN MATHEMATICS

In what follows we shall focus on the standard of the élite in the in-dustrialized IEA countries, using as our criteria achievements in math-ematics and science at the pre-university level. The national systems which have been studied vary considerably with regard to retention rate or "holding power" at the upper secondary level. The high school seniors consist of some 75 per cent of the relevant age group in the United States, those who finish *gymnasium* and continuation school in Sweden (grades 11 and 12) are some 45 per cent of the age group, the *Oberprimaner* (grade 13) in the Federal Republic of Germany are some 10 per cent etc. It is rather pointless to limit a comparison of student achievements in these and other countries to mean performances, simply because of the highly variable portion of the relevant age group we are dealing with. It is more nearly fair to compare *equal portions* of the age cohorts.

But such comparisons are conducted under the assumption that those who are *not* in school at that age level have not, either by previous schooling or other learning opportunities, reached the level of competence achieved by the élite still in school. On the basis of analysis of the distributions of achievements, both at the beginning and at the end of secondary school, we concluded that had the ideal conditions of being able to test the entire age group existed those who were not in school would not have scored high enough to affect the means for the top 5 per cent of the age group.

The objection has been raised that the method of comparing equal portions of the age group is unfair to national systems with a low retention rate (or high selectivity). The validity of such an objection can be questioned on pure logical grounds, simply because it is not consistent with the élitist philosophy. In systems where until recently only some 5–15 per cent of the entire age group is retained up to the pre-university grade, the prevailing educational philosophy has been that such a system rather efficiently takes care of most of the able pupils and does not bias against any category of them. Thus, those who favour an élitist system cannot reasonably object to a comparison between equal proportions of the age group by maintaining that the comparison is unfair to the selective system because it does not retain the able pupils. There is, however, a valid statistical objection. Härnqvist (1974) in reviewing the IEA surveys in science, reading and literature points out that the errors of measurement contribute to an overestimation of the size standard of the élite in comprehensive systems and conversely to an underestimation in selective systems.

When in the IEA mathematics study (Husén, 1967) the average performance in different countries of terminal students taking mathematics was compared, we found that the US high school graduates were far below the other countries. However, in the US 18 per cent of the age group of 17–18 year olds took mathematics as compared to

Figure 1. *Mean Mathematics Test Scores (1) for the Total Sample and (2) for equal Proportions of Age Group in Each Country for Terminal Mathematics Populations*

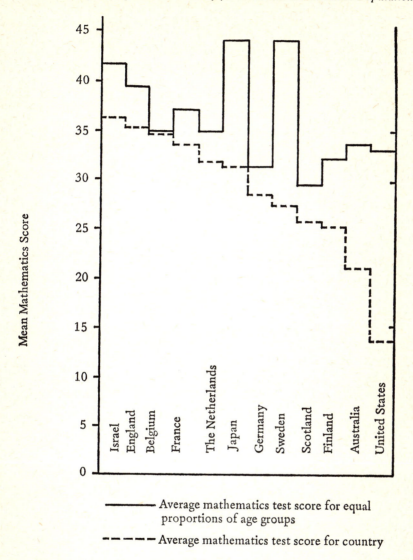

Average mathematics test score for equal
proportions of age groups

– – – – – Average mathematics test score for country

Source: T. Husén (Ed.): International Study of Achievement in Mathematics: A
Comparison Between Twelve Countries. New York: Wiley, 1967.

Figure 2. *Percent of Age Group Reaching Upper Tenth of Terminal Mathematics Pupils by International Standards*

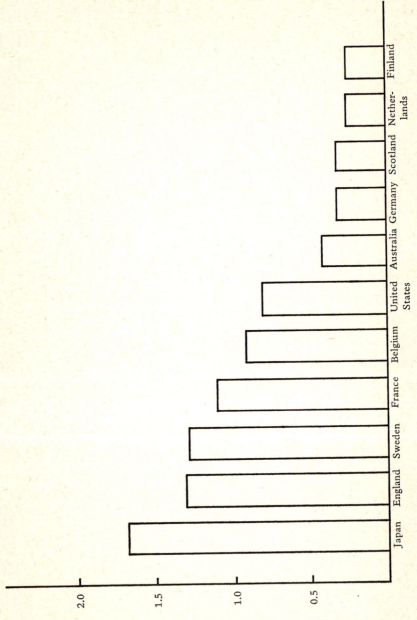

Source: T. Husén (Ed.): International Study of Achievement in Mathematics: A Comparison Between Twelve Countries. New York: Wiley, 1967.

4–5 per cent in some European countries. In order to arrive at an answer to the question to what extent it is possible to produce an élite in a comprehensive system, one has to compare equal proportions of the relevant age group in the respective countries. The dotted line in Figure 1 gives the average performance of the terminal mathematics student in the twelve countries. The solid line gives the averages for the top four percent of the total age group. This percentage was selected because it represented the lowest proportion in any one country taking mathematics. As can be seen, the range between countries is more narrow than for the entire group of terminal mathematics pupils. The United States' top four percent score at about the same level as the corresponding group in other countries.

On the basis of the distribution of total score of the terminal pupils in all countries, international percentile norms were obtained. In Figure 2 we have given the percentage of the total age group within each country which has reached the standard of the upper tenth of the terminal mathematics pupils. As can be seen, none of the systems with high retention rates and/or a comprehensive structure are among the five systems at the bottom.

STANDARD OF THE ELITE IN SCIENCE

Similar comparisons were conducted with terminal students in science (Comber and Keeves, 1973). In this case all the Population 4 pupils were included in the comparisons, irrespective of whether they were or were not taking science in the grade when testing took place. It was decided to compare the top 9 per cent of Population 4 in the industrialized countries. This percentage was chosen because it represented the lowest proportion in Population 4 of the relevant age group in any of the countries. In order to arrive at measures of two more limited élites, the top 5 and 1 per cent were also chosen. Table 5 and Figure 3 present the outcomes of the comparisons for the three élite groups. The mean score for the entire graduate population ranges from 30.8 for New Zealand to only 14.2 for the United States. As can be seen in Table 5, the Population 4 pupils represent 13 per cent of the entire age group in the former country as compared to 75 in the latter. When the mean scores for the top 9 per cent were compared, it was found that countries with a high retention rate got sharply increased means. The United States doubled its mean and scored higher than, for instance, Germany and France. By and large the same picture emerged when countries

Figure 3. *Science Mean Scores of Top 1%, Top 5%, Top 9% of an Age-Group and of Overall Group*

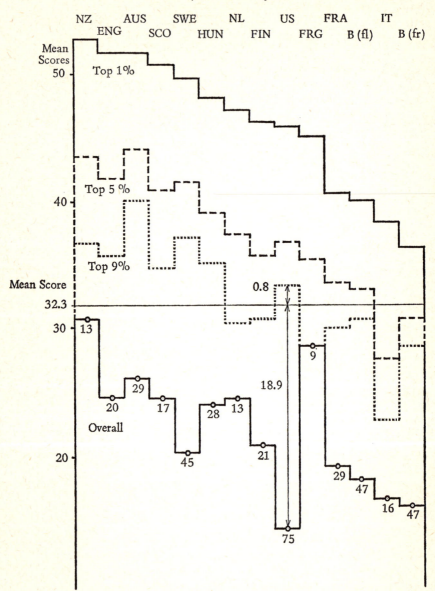

Source: L. C. Comber and John P. Keeves: Science Education in Nineteen Countries. Stockholm and New York: Almqvist & Wiksell and Wiley-Halsted Press, 1973.

TABLE 5: *Means and Standard Deviations for Science Test Scores for Total Sample and Equivalent Proportions of an Age Group*

Country	% at School	N	Full Sample Mean	SD	Top 1% Mean	SD	Top 5% Mean	SD	Top 9% Mean	SD
New Zealand	13	1 676	30.8	12.6	52.8	2.8	43.5	5.9	36.8	9.0
England	20	2 181	24.4	12.4	51.6	3.2	41.6	6.5	35.5	8.5
Australia	29	4 194	26.1	11.5	51.5	3.2	44.0	4.7	39.9	5.9
Scotland	17	1 321	24.4	12.9	50.7	3.8	40.6	6.4	34.4	8.7
Sweden	45	2 754	20.1	10.9	49.5	3.4	41.2	5.3	37.0	6.2
Hungary	28	2 828	24.0	9.6	48.0	3.8	39.0	5.4	35.0	6.1
Netherlands	13	1 138	24.4	12.0	47.1	3.6	37.2	6.5	30.3	9.4
Finland	21	1 725	20.8	10.5	46.0	4.1	35.7	6.4	30.7	7.4
USA	75	2 514	14.2	9.9	45.8	2.8	36.8	5.5	33.1	5.9
FRG	9	1 989	28.4	9.6	45.0	4.1	35.3	6.2	28.4	9.6
France	29	3 523	19.1	9.1	40.5	3.5	33.3	4.4	29.9	5.1
Belgium (Fl)	47	467	18.1	8.5	39.8	3.7	33.0	4.0	30.5	4.2
Italy	16	15 719	16.5	9.2	38.2	4.7	27.4	6.5	22.7	7.3
Belgium (Fr)	47	941	16.0	8.3	36.2	2.0	30.9	3.1	28.4	3.7
Average			22.0		45.9		37.1		32.3	
Range			16.6		16.6		16.6		17.2	
Chile	16	1 947	9.3	6.3	23.5	3.8	16.8	4.3	13.6	4.8
India	14	3 040	6.3	6.1	20.8	3.7	12.8	4.8	9.5	5.2
Iran	9	1 051	10.8	5.9	21.9	3.6	14.8	4.4	10.8	5.9
Thailand	10	724	12.5	6.1	23.2	2.4	17.4	3.6	13.6	5.3

were compared with regard to the top 5 and 1 per cent of the students.

The assessment of the standard of élite pupils at the pre-university level does not support the contention that systems with broader or more open access and with relative high retention rate until the end of upper secondary school do not succeed in "producing" élite pupils. An élite can be cultivated with a comprehensive educational system. Whether or not an élite produced in the latter system is worth its price is another question.

In selective systems the high standard of the élite is often bought at the price of limiting opportunities of the mass of the pupils. By comparing the distribution of father's occupation at the 14-year-old level with the one at the pre-university level, it is possible within each country to arrive at an estimation of the amount of social selection that operates between the two levels. An index of social disproportion was derived from the proportion of pupils with fathers who belonged to the professional and managerial category on one hand and the semi-skilled or unskilled category on the other. The index was unity when the upper and lower strata have the same representation at the pre-university level as at the 14-year-old level. The index was 1.3 and 2.4 respectively for the United States and Sweden, two countries with relatively comprehensive and retentive systems; whereas it was 7.9 for England and as high as 37.7 for the Federal Republic of Germany, where the systems are much more selective and less retentive. An index of dissimilarity between socio-economic strata developed by Anderson (1967) gives by and large the same results. Table 6 gives the percentages for the two contrasted status categories. Since the categorization has not been consistent over countries, comparisons should be made *between* levels *within* countries. One should notice the low representation in England and the Federal Republic of Germany of pupils with working class background at the pre-university level.

TABLE 6: *Percentage of Pupils Within Each Population From Selected Categories of Parental Occupation*

	Population I (10-year-olds)		Population II (14-year-olds)		Population IV (17-19 year-olds)	
	Profes- sional & Mana- gerial	*Unskilled & semi- skilled workers*	*Profes- sional & Mana- gerial*	*Unskilled & semi- skilled workers*	*Profes- sional & Mana- gerial*	*Unskilled & semi- skilled workers*
England	16	21	14	14	38	5
Fed. Rep. of Germany	13	7	14	8	49	1
Finland	9	35	10	34	20	15
Hungary	15	43	20	36	38	18
Netherlands	26	12	20	12	55	5
Sweden	23	31	26	27	35	15
USA	24	18	31	16	34	14

Source: L. C. Comber and John P. Keeves: Science Education in Nineteen Countries. Stockholm and New York: Almqvist & Wiksell and Wiley-Halsted Press, 1973.

The overall conclusion from the comparisons is that the comprehensive system, by its openness, lack of selective examinations during the primary and initial secondary school period and its high retention rate, is a more effective strategy in taking care of all the talent of a nation. By casting the net as widely as possible an attempt is made to "catch" an optimum number of fish. A selective system with early separation of pupils who are rated to have academic potential is destined to produce good end products. But this advantage is bought at the high price of excluding a sizeable number of pupils from lower class homes from further education and of limiting the opportunities for the great mass of pupils to get access to quality education.

CHAPTER 8

CONSTRAINTS ON THE DEVELOPMENT OF TALENT

INTRODUCTORY OBSERVATIONS

According to the classical liberal conception of the utilization of talent the individual is born with a certain endowment – his "native wit" – which he primarily is responsible for developing to its full potential. There should be no artificial barriers in the institutional system of education to bar him from taking advantage of the opportunities his abilities entitle him to. Equal opportunity in a formal sense should be given to everybody by removing economic, social and geographic barriers which prevent the able from climbing the educational ladder ("*freie Bahn der Tüchtigen*"). A key idea in this philosophy is that talent is mainly inborn, something that squares with the view of divine destiny. The active participation of the individual in molding his own fate squares with the Protestant work ethic. Those who succeed and those who fail get the praise and the blame for effort or lack of effort respectively. Thus, as Michael Young (1958) spells out in his parable, $M = E \times A$, merit equals effort times ability. In a system where everybody tries hard to develop himself, a "natural aristocracy", to use Jefferson's phrase, will replace the ascriptive nobility.

In the Western world this conception translated into practical politics means that able young people from lower classes should get the support they need in order to enter institutions of higher education. This kind of philosophy was further developed by several liberal thinkers in Europe during the 19th century. The Swedish Count Torsten Rudenschiöld in 1845 published a much debated book titled *Thoughts Concerning Mobility Between the Estates (Tankar om ståndscirkulation)*. He envisaged a society wherein school education would serve as the ideal allocator of status according to individual capacity. Maximum social mobility would be guaranteed not only by seeing to it that able young people from lower classes were given opportunities

to move up the educational ladder but also by assigning those with
limited capacities from upper classes to the minimum formal education from which they could then move into humble occupations.
Rudenschiöld, in fact, played an important role in developing the
idea that the elementary school should be common during mandatory
school attendance to all social classes, which has remained a key policy
issue in Swedish as well as in other West European educational policy
far into the 20th century. By making basic education "comprehensive"
and undifferentiated in terms of curricula, and also, foremost, by
enrolling all the children from a given "catching area", the promotion
of children at all levels of ability would be optimized.

The assumption has been that greater equalization of educational
opportunities will in its wake have enhanced equalization of *life
chances*, not only of chances for advanced education. But the power of
the formal school system to act as an equalizer is, as is evident from
quite a few surveys conducted during the 60's and 70's, in fact more
limited than has been anticipated (Husén, 1972). In a keynote address
at the OECD Conference in 1970 on Policies for Educational Growth,
Ingvar Carlsson, then Minister of Education in Sweden, had the
following to say about "education as a promotor of social change":

"It is possible that we have been too optimistic, particularly perhaps concerning the time it takes to bring about changes. On the other hand it is
hardly possible to change society only through education. To equalize educational opportunities without influencing working conditions, the setting
of wage rates, etc. in other ways, would easily become an empty gesture.
The reforms of educational policy must go together with reforms in other
fields: labour market policy, economic policy, social policy, fiscal policy,
etc." (OECD, 1971c, p. 69).

In their summary report on the conference Frankel and Halsey concluded:

"Too much has been claimed for the power of educational systems as instruments for the wholesale reform of societies which are characteristically
hierarchical in their distribution of chances in life as between races, classes,
the sexes and as between metropolitan/suburban and provincial/rural populations. The typical history of educational expansion in the 1950's and 1960's
for the OECD countries can be represented by a graph of inequality of attainment between the above-mentioned social categories which has shifted
markedly upwards without changing its slope. In other words, relative
chances have not altered materially despite expansion" (*ibid.*, p. 14).

The role of the formal educational system in a society at a high level of technology and in a dynamic movement toward further utilization of technology is first and foremost to impart certain common basic skills and knowledge – a task which in our complex society takes a longer and longer time for the individual to absorb – upon which are then built certain competencies that are "marketable" in specific occupations. The formal educational system is there, then, not primarily to equalize but to differentiate competencies. But the great differentiator in our society, as has been repeatedly shown by extensive national and international surveys (Coleman, 1966; Plowden, 1967; Husén, 1967; Comber and Keeves, 1973), is the family (including the genetic assets) and the social matrix at large in which the child grows up. Basic cognitive differences have to a large extent developed by the time the child enters primary school. As shown in the surveys, at all levels of the formal educational system the proportions of the between-pupil differences accounted for by the home are much larger than those accounted for by the school resources and the teaching-learning process going on there.

STRUCTURAL CHARACTERISTICS ACTING AS RESTRAINTS

The aim of this chapter is to try to map out some of the constraints on the promotion of talent that are inherent in the educational system *per se*. As pointed out above and spelled out more fully in another context (Husén, 1972) the mere fact that the system has as its main objective the imparting of certain competencies in terms of study skills, specific bits of knowledge and certain social rituals makes it basically selective. The only question is *how* selective the system has to be. This is chiefly depending upon its prevailing structure and teaching practices.

In the first place we have to consider the overall *structure* of the formal educational system and the mechanisms of selection, sorting, and differentiation which are to a large extent determined by that structure. As noted in an earlier chapter, a key issue in West European school policy in this century has been its structural dualism. The establishment of compulsory elementary schools in the 19th century created two school systems which at the beginning were completely parallel to each other. On the one hand there was a compulsory school which enrolled children from lower social strata and on the other a university-preparing, academically-oriented school serving children from upper social strata who obtained their grounding for the secondary school in private preparatory schools. The compulsory, tax-supported elementary school was a product of the 19th century, whereas the university-preparing school had a long tradition going back to the medieval Latin school. The first problem faced by those who wanted to reform the system was that of building a bridge, however narrow it might be, between the two systems. In Sweden, for example, a link-up whereby it was possible to transfer from the elementary school to the first grade in the secondary school was not established until 1894. A child who had completed the so-called A-type elementary school could transfer to the first grade in the secondary school, but that type of school for a long time recruited the bulk of its pupils from private preparatory schools (Husén, 1962).

Prolonged compulsory school attendance meant an increase in years the common primary school and the selective academic secondary school ran parallel to each other. Since transfer to the academic secondary school in many West European countries traditionally has taken place – and still takes place – at the age of 10–12, increasing numbers of young people of compulsory school age 10–15 are getting an education which in several respects has different aims from those of the academically-oriented schools. It is pertinent to recall here that the Swedish Minister of Education, in stating the terms of reference for the 1940 Royal Commission of inquiry into school reform, underlined the dilemma posed by a continually enlarged system of parallelism. Apart from the purely educational drawbacks entailed in such a system at the upper level of the primary school, it had serious implications for a policy of equalization of opportunities. The same problem impinged itself on government or other committees assigned to deal with structural matters in the Federal Republic of Germany, England, and France (OECD, 1971a, 1972).

Until well into the 1950's the school systems of many West European countries, such as Britain, France and Germany, consisted of two almost completely distinct subsystems: a primary school for all and a secondary school for a social and intellectual élite. Transfers from one system to the other occurred with few exceptions at the ages 10 or 11. For the large majority of pupils this meant that a decision was made for them then which determined their entire life career. Those who were admitted to the lower section of the academic secondary school after the first few grades in the primary school were heading for the more prestigious and better paid positions within the broad spectrum of so-called white-collar jobs. Those who remained in the upper grades of the primary school until completion of compulsory schooling were as a rule consigned to manual labor. In several countries until recently the secondary university-preparing school (for instance the *Gymnasium* in Germany and the *lycée* in France) has provided a continuous course *en bloc* from the age of 10 or 11 until age 18 or 19.

At the beginning of this century several countries established a middle school to provide education for those workers who needed education additional to that afforded by the elementary school. The middle school could also pave the way to the upper secondary school which more directly prepared for university entry.

The tendency in Western Europe during the last few decades has been to move toward integration of various school types or tracks within schools which for a number of grades run parallel to each other. In cases where the compulsory tax-supported elementary school was accepted as preparatory to the pre-university school, the pupils were as a rule not older than 10 or 11 when they transferred. A considerable portion of the pupils were recruited from private, preparatory schools. Concurrent with the efforts to strengthen compulsory schooling by enriching its programs and duration, attempts were made to set off the lower grades of the pre-university school into a separate middle school. Thus a definitive allocation into academic and non-academic tracks would be postponed until the age of 15–16, which would also postpone a split into definitive occupational categories.

The gradual introduction of universal secondary schooling concomitant with a prolongation of compulsory schooling has results in various organizational solutions, the main features of which will be briefly outlined here. Three different types of solution can be distinguished, though they are by no means mutually exclusive.

(1) National systems with a primary stage serving all pupils up to the age of 10–12, and with a middle stage that is partly integrated, partly selective. Pertinent examples, though to a varying extent, are the systems in England, France, and the Federal Republic of Germany. The 1944 Education Act in England made secondary school universal up to the age of 15, but entailed provisions for a rather definitive "allocation" of pupils on the basis of examinations at the age of 11. Until recently only a few regional school systems had "gone comprehensive". There is a general tendency to lessen the rigor of the so-called eleven-plus examination. A strongly established private secondary school

system is still in existence, and has an enrollment from upper social strata and better resources than the tax-supported system (Pidgeon, 1967).

The reforms implemented or projected in France and Germany have considerably modified the selective or differentiating features of the middle grades, i.e., those serving the ages 10–11 through 16. The 1959 decree in France lengthened compulsory schooling by two years, from age 14 to 16. At the same time provisions were made for an "observation stage" (*cycle d'observation*) before pupils are definitively allocated to one or another type of secondary school. The rapid expansion of *collèges d'enseignement général*, which according to 1963 legislation are part of basic education, *enseignement du premier degré*, contributed to making the middle grades much less selective (OECD, 1971b). A similar development, although less marked, has been taking place in Germany. The age of 10 is still strategic, since it signifies the transition from *Grundschule* to *Hauptschule*. Those children whose parents apply for their entry into *Mittelschule* and *Gymnasium* have to take an entrance course organized in cooperation between teachers of the delivering and the receiving school. In several *Länder* (States) experiments are being carried out with a "promotion stage" (*Förderstufe*) the aim of which is similar to that of the "observation stage" in France, namely to postpone a definitive allocation to a program from age 10 or 11 to some time later (Hüfner, 1973). New types of upper secondary schools have sprung up in these two countries alongside the prestigious classical *lycée* or *Gymnasium*, so that the humanistic-classical pre-university school no longer holds a monopoly on entry into the professions.

(2) Some national systems have tried to solve the problem of parallelism by setting up a middle school or a stage above the primary stage as part of the compulsory system. This has, as indicated above, recently been done in France by setting up the *collèges d'enseignement général*. The result is to eliminate any single institution that carries its pupils all the way on through the secondary school, from grade 5 or 6 as had long been the case in England, France, and Germany. For a long time the only countries with a middle school system were the Scandinavian ones and the Netherlands. Transfers to the pre-university school were thus deferred to the age of 15 or 16. Sweden discarded that system definitively by its Education Act of 1962, which made the 9-year basic school common to all children through ages 7 to 16.

Whereas in the first category, as described above, the types of schools that cover the ages 11–13 are part of the secondary school system, in the second category they become integrated into the primary school system. In a way it could be said that those systems with a "fluid" middle stage are in the process of transition to the third stage, that of a fully integrated basic school covering the entire compulsory school attendance period.

(3) In some national or regional systems all the children and all the curricular programs of the compulsory school period are to be found in the same institutional framework. Different labels with varying degrees of overlap have been given to this kind of organization: *Einheitsschule*, "comprehensive school", *école unique*, *grundskola*, *Gesamtschule*. Thus, the unitary system providing basic education through ages 7 to 16 was introduced in Sweden during the 1950's on a pilot basis, and since 1962 has operated full-scale. A *Gesamtschule* is under way on a pilot basis in the state of Hesse in Germany. Legislation in recent years in Finland and Norway has set up the same kind of provisions as were established earlier in Sweden.

There is little doubt that the West European countries are moving toward restructuring their national systems so as to place the stage of education that coincides with the mandatory school attendance period in one common type of institution. The great obstacle to change has been the demarcation line at the age of 10 or 11, when transfer to selective academic education traditionally has taken place. This has been such a deeply ingrained institutional feature, reinforced by so much vested interest, that it suffices as an explanation for the great reform inertia that can be noticed over the last 25 years in such countries as England and Germany (Hüfner, 1973). As costs for education rise and doubts begin to grow about the worthwhileness of institutionalized education for teenagers, this inertia becomes fortified.

There are certain factors, however, which will contribute to molding national systems in the direction of unitary institutions for the compulsory school period. The demand for increased equality of opportunity (*Chancengleichheit*) or "democratization" of education is concomitant with the demand for a more open and flexible system entailing a minimum of selection hurdles, at least at the secondary level. Furthermore, increasing economic development will unremittingly increase the demand for skilled manpower, which in turn will put pressure on the educational system to increase intake at more advanced levels. Thirdly, a higher level of "consumption" of education follows from a higher standard of living. Young people no longer need to contribute to the household, either by working at home or through gainful employment outside, and the structure of the economy makes it increasingly difficult for them to find jobs. These factors together account for the "enrollment explosion" that has taken place on both sides of the Atlantic during the last few decades, although in some European countries it did not come about until the 1960's.

Sooner or later there is for the individual a decisive turning point as regards advanced education. As brought out above, until recently institutionalized selection has taken place as early as at age 10 or 11. The surveys conducted by the International Association for the Evaluation of Educational Achievements showed that the earlier the selection takes place, the more biased it is against children from lower-class or low-educated origins (Husén, 1967, 1973; Postlethwaite, 1967; Pidgeon, 1967). An organizational feature that has often been overlooked is the degree of differentiation between parallel programs and the rigidity of the differentiation as evidenced by the degree of difficulty in moving from one to another. If at the secondary level there are clearly differentiated programs, such as the purely academic and the purely vocational, the "permeability" between programs tends to become almost entirely one-way: from the academic to the vocational. Even highly developed guidance programs are unable to overcome this one-sidedness (Husén, 1962). The overall explanation is that the academic program is more prestigious and keeps more options open at subsequent levels. Those who have entered the vocational program reduce considerably their range of options in terms of advanced education. Since lower class parents hold lower aspirations for their children than do upper class parents, the likelihood of a child from the former category entering the academic program is much lower than for a child in the latter category, other factors, such as marks, examination scores, etc., being equal.

GROUPING AND TEACHING PRACTICES ACTING AS RESTRAINTS

An outstanding feature even of those systems which organizationally have been "unitary" or comprehensive has often been *grouping practices* whereby a certain amount of homogeneity is secured. Closely related to this is the practice of referring to special classes children who are diagnosed as retarded. School readiness tests have been used, and are still widely used, to assess mainly the cognitive competence of the child who according to age is ready to enter primary school. The fact that lower class children are highly overrepresented among those who score low on the "school readiness" tests, and therefore either have to defer entry or are referred to special classes for the less ready, should serve as a warning signal against social discrimination (Johansson, 1965). The role expectation subtly, though seldom explicitly, conveyed to children referred to special classes, especially classes for the so-called retarded, is that they are "out of the race".

More serious social implications of grouping practices come from the "streaming" or "homogeneous grouping" system. Jackson (1964) surveyed the streaming practice at the primary level in England. He could clearly establish two important effects. In the first place, the quality or rank of the stream was highly correlated with social background, and secondly, those who were assigned to the lower stream were out of the competition when it came to being admitted to the more demanding programs at the secondary level.

In a way, the practice of allocating children so as to achieve greater group homogeneity, which is supposed to benefit both the able and the dull, is an attempt to regain at the classroom level what has been lost at the level of overall structure in terms of having different types of schools for different types of pupils.

The "norm-referenced" approach that has so far characterized the European school systems – that is, children's performances are ranked and each child's achievements are evaluated not against any criterion of "goal-attainment" but against some kind of mean or percentile – has reinforced the tendency to establish homogeneity by grouping.

One practice that to a widely varying extent has been traditionally employed in Europe is *grade-repeating*.

Girard (1953) and Girard and Bastides (1969) have conducted surveys on the flow of students through the French system according to their social origin. According to a study by Girard, Bastides and Pourcher (1963) there are striking differences between the pupils from various socio-economic strata with regard to the academic rating given them by their teachers and their age (which reflects grade-repeating). About twice as many children whose parents are professionals and executives are of or under the normal age than are children whose parents are manual workers or farmers. The flow charts referred to in the OECD review of French educational policy (OECD, 1971b) show that grade-repeating is not only high but significantly correlated with social status of parents. This means, then, that already in the primary cycle those of lower class background become disqualified to enter the competition for the academic tracks at the secondary level. This handicap is then accumulated up to the university level, where the representation of lower class students is very low.

Two follow-up studies with the aim of elucidating grade-repeating in Sweden were conducted by Royal Commissions in the lower secondary school (*realskola*), in both cases on fairly representative national samples. The first study was conducted on the intake of 1938, which was followed until 1944 (SOU, 1944). The second, focused on the 1953 intake, was followed for six years (Orring, 1959). It should be noted that this was a selective school which in the 1930's, on the basis of entrance examinations, admitted less than 15 per cent of an age cohort. From 1938 to 1953 the intake more than doubled, but the rates of grade-repeating and dropout were almost exactly remained the same.

Formal certificates of admission to institutions of higher learning serve as unjustified constraints, insofar as the qualifications certified may in some respects bear little or no relationship to the requirements the students have to meet in the receiving institution. The reason the matriculation examination was abolished in Sweden in 1968 was simply that the institutions of higher learning had become so diversified that a uniform entrance ticket in terms of a secondary school certificate based on a matriculation examination had gradually become meaningless, particularly since some university faculties had adopted a *numerus clausus* system with diverse admission requirements that were supposed to meet their particular demands.

In the long run the concept of recurrent education and decreased emphasis on extensive package courses leading up to degrees for the great majority of students will open up institutions of higher learning to *ad hoc* needs which previously could not be met.

SEX DIFFERENCES

Sex differences in participation in further education, in spite of the frequently documented fact that there are no sex differences in general intelligence that cannot be accounted for by environmental conditions, indicate that women more often than men do not have the opportunity to realize their potentiality in the educational system (OECD, 1970). When it comes to specialized abilities, such as the spatial and the verbal, there appears to be some interaction between sex-linked genetic factors and socio-cultural factors (Maccoby, 1966 and 1973). In the IEA Project in science there were clear sex differences in achievement already at the age of 10. These differences increased considerably up to the pre-university level, at which point they were very high for physics but rather moderate for biology. Since item analysis data are available for each country and age level, a detailed scrutiny might reveal to what extent differences can be attributed to the teaching and the content of science curricula (Comber and Keeves, 1973).

CONCLUDING REMARKS

Educational systems have to a varying extent built-in mechanisms which exert restraints in terms of promoting the development of talent and are biased against students of disadvantaged background. The chances for lower class students to reach higher levels of education are particularly small in systems where selective procedures in terms of "streaming" or grade-repeating are employed already at the primary level.

The overriding policy issue particularly in the West European educational systems during the last few decades has been the abolition of an early transfer from the elementary school to the university-preparing secondary school by merging the two systems at the lower secondary level. The longer this transfer (and the selection procedures that go with it) can be postponed the greater the chances for children of lower class families to reach the upper secondary and the university level.

CHAPTER 9

IMPLICATIONS FOR LONG-RANGE
STRATEGY IN EDUCATION

Appropriate utilization of talent has increasingly come to be regarded as the "wealth of nations", developed and developing alike. Educated talent is part and parcel of the building up of a sophisticated technology and the increasingly complicated coordination and administration which goes with it. Basic formal education for the masses and advanced education that can create the leadership are necessary prerequisites for bringing about so-called modernization of countries in the Third World. But educated talent is regarded not only as a national asset. It is also seen as a means of enhancing the life chances of the individual and of boosting his earning power. Education has for some time been conceived of as giving higher rates of return than other types of capital investment.

The quest for "democratization" of further education, referred to by some economists as increased educational consumption or "social demand" for education, has been the other force behind the expansion of formal educational systems all over the world, not least in Europe. Democratization of education conceived during the period from 1918 up to the 1960's simply meant that every pupil, regardless of social background and geographical location, should have the same opportunity to pursue further education (which usually meant upper secondary and university education) once he had demonstrated his ability.

To define scholastic ability seemed for a long time to be a relatively simple matter. School marks, test scores. and examinations showed who was worthy of being promoted. But once it became apparent that these criteria were correlated with social background, the matter of "equality of opportunity" did not seem so simple any longer. For one thing, what is *meant* by "talent" or "ability" is in the long run determined by the prevailing social values. "Talent" or "ability" is defined in any one particular socio-cultural context by social criteria which are especially valued because they are conducive to success, i.e., to high status, which does not necessarily (as seems to be assumed, for instance, by Jencks, 1972) mean pecuniary rewards. In talking about "talent" in the context of education we imply the cognitive skills and competencies that are conducive to successful climbing on the educational ladder in the "learning society".

"Talent", in the debate that has been taking place on both sides of the Atlantic, is usually identified with IQ, which is an index of scholastic ability since most so-called IQ tests have been validated against criteria of scholastic performance, such as marks, teacher ratings or examination results. Since talent conceived of as scholastic ability increasingly has tended to condition social status and mobility, the question of the extent to which it is determined by genetic factors has become crucial. The issue is epitomized in Richard Herrnstein's (1971) famous syllogism: If differences in IQ are inherited, if success requires high ability, and if status and earnings define success, then social status will to some extent depend on inherited differences in IQ. The passion of the debate, of course, reflects the fact that the two conceptions, the hereditarian and the environmental, often are imbedded in two opposing social philosophies. The hereditarian view is often wedded to the opinion that apart from minor adjustments society is in no need of being changed. The position an individual has reached on the whole reflects the capacity laid down in him by destiny. Therefore, the social stratification we have is a reasonable one. The environmental view has close affinity with a more radical conception of desirable changes in modern society. In an address to an audience of sociologists, Faris (1961) advanced the conviction that "the amount of ability in each person is created in the course of experience, and the supply of ability in any society is at present a consequence mainly of impersonal social processes rather than intentional control" (p. 838). Those who have taken a strong hereditarian stance have sided with those who oppose structural changes in the educational system from an élitist and selective to a comprehensive one.

Anyhow, individual differences, be they mainly genetic or mainly environmental, give rise to problems of social equality and meritocracy. How can we "democratize" education in the face of initial diversity in scholastic ability, regardless of how these differences are mainly determined? This is a dilemma already looming large in the highly industrial society of today, and the indications are that it will beset even more the post-industrial society. How can the principle of equality of opportunity be made compatible with inherent tendencies toward meritocracy?

Since the focus of this monograph is on the availability of talent, two major problems are: What should we mean by "pool of talent"? And can this pool be quantitatively assessed? For a long time those, as a rule of lower class background, with good scholastic aptitude who were not found in institutions of furthergoing education were referred to as "the reserve of talent". This conception was built on the tacit assumption of a once and for all given, mainly inherited capital of talent which to a varying extent could be developed or "tapped". As can be seen from the summing up of the development of the methodology employed in measuring the non-utilized talent, this research has had important repercussions on the theoretical conceptions, such as to raise questions regarding the extent to which the "capital" of talent could be increased by planned social policy.

The question of the national supply of talent was once, in the 1930's, dramatized by a book title referring to the "fight" for the national intelligence. In England, surveys in which group intelligence tests were given to school children showed that IQ as measured by the tests was negatively correlated with family size. It was negatively correlated with social class as well. The basic problem was whether and to what extent the intelligence capital was diminishing as a result of differential fertility. Therefore, the heredity-environmental issue was at the core of the debate. In the 1940's an extensive survey research in England, partly under the auspices of the Eugenics Society, was conducted and further material bearing on the problem of intelligence and differential fertility was available at the World Population Conference in Rome in 1954. Eventually, the testing of representative groups after an interval of 13 to 15 years indicated an increased instead of a decreased mean phenotypic intelligence level, which was the opposite of the prediction in the 1930's. In focusing on this as well as on other problems of talent, the research endeavors became more sophisticated from both a conceptual and a methodological point of view. An attempt has been made in this book to write up in a separate chapter the story of how the dilemma of predicted decline and observed rise was resolved.

The issue as to whether the potential intellectual capital is in the process of being gradually destroyed by (alleged) higher fertility among less intelligent, lower class individuals is by no means just an academic one. It has vast policy implications. The dual assumptions that differences in test scores are indicators of differences in inborn intelligence and that those who score low on these tests reproduce in greater numbers than those who score high, lead to certain eugenic conclusions which in some countries have for a long time been implemented by certain regulations about sterilization. The author, who during the 1940's worked as a psychologist in the Swedish Armed Services, and in that capacity was responsible for the construction of the Classification Test administered to all conscripts at the age of 20, experienced the following case. A young man who appeared before one of the Conscription Boards was interviewed by one of the psychologists. He told of having been sent as a child to an institution for the mentally retarded. At the end of his stay he was seen briefly by a psychiatrist who gave him a test which according to the recollection of the young man, appears to have been the Stanford-Binet test, and who then subjected the young man to sterilization. His score on the Classification Test, which was a group test with predominantly verbal items, corresponded to an IQ of close to 100. The case reached the press and gave rise to a lively public debate on the heredity-environment issue (Husén, 1961).

Taking cognizance of the fact that formal schooling "boosts" IQ, as assessed by conventional intelligence tests which measure the type of skills that are crystallizations of cognitive habits and strategies partly learned at school, it is reasonable to assume that, other things being equal, it is the prolonged schooling experience that has enhanced the intellectual competence as measured by the tests. Furthermore, the extra-scholastic experiences from mass media, such as radio and television, plus all the increased exposure to verbal material at home, can be assumed to have "raised" the IQ throughout the period when not only has the "enrollment explosion" been most intense but the electronic communication media have become commonplace in homes. On top of this, we have had in many countries substantial improvements in child care, in nutrition practices, and in the public welfare.

The group convened by UNESCO in 1954 made the following statement: "Although recognizing the limiting effects of genetic factors, the group emphasizes the possibilities of an increase in intellectual competence through the improvement of environmental opportunities. In particular, there is in each country a considerable reservoir of intelligence which might be brought to greater social use through an extension of educational opportunities without distinction as to sex, social origin or ethnic background" (United Nations, 1955).

Until recently in most West European countries, roughly 50 to 80 per cent of the children of professional and upper managerial background qualified for university entrance by completing the upper secondary academic school, as compared to 1 to 2 per cent, among those of working class or farming background. Even assuming that genetic dispositions for the kind of behavior required to reach that level of education are not randomly distributed among the social classes but due to assortive mating are somewhat amassed in the upper classes (something that a geneticist such as Dobzhansky, 1973, doubts), such a tremendous imbalance in participation in higher education could not be accounted for by social class differences in genetic dispositions. As noted above (p. 51), a projected increase of the matriculants from 5 to 20 per cent of the relevant age group in Sweden would in 1946 have been regarded as a most ridiculous estimate. The majority of those in Western and Northern Europe who are now qualifying for university entrance have a lower class background. In this respect the expansion of enrollment has benefited the "reserve" of ability available in those strata, where young people previously had very limited access to further education. But, as has been stressed in several connections, "reserve" should not be interpreted to mean that there is a fixed intellectual capital, defined entirely by the genes conditioning intellectual development (cf. Halsey, 1961). It is, in a sense, a social capital which can be increased substantially by the way it is put to work. The intellectual capacity a person displays is, in a strict sense, not anything that he "has" as an individual. Within the confines of certain genetic dispositions that he partly shares with his family, his intellectual development depends on the kind of interaction he has with parents, siblings, peers and others. This, in the last analysis, depends on the kind of society he grows up in.

The author is of the opinion that in framing strategies and in defining goals and actions for education in the future one has for pragmatic reasons to take an environmental stance based upon the conviction that education can bring about certain worthwhile changes in pupils. The educator has got to be an "environmentalist" if he wants to justify his existence. This means, then, that the behavioral scientist who would provide the educator with a knowledge base for action should focus his efforts on what specific environmental factors can do in modifying pupils' behaviour instead of devoting his interest to what the genetic limitations are. The genetic factors cannot be directly observed and assessed but have to be inferred from a study of the process of development under specific developmental conditions. The more successful we become in assessing the tangible, i.e. the various environmental variables and the behaviors related to them, the more of the observed individual differences we can attribute to environment. What is left after we have taken into account the tangible, can be referred to as innate. We can thus become more accurate in mapping out the limitations set by internal influences, which may then be properly referred to as genetic. The point is that we should in the first place try to find out what can be done, instead of investigating the conditions which, when we are dealing with human behavior, are so elusive as are the genetic ones.

The "pool of talent" of a nation in terms of the developmental potential of general and specialized intelligence that can be deployed is, therefore, not determined once and for all by the gene pool. Breeding across national and class boundaries in the type of society prevailing in Western Europe occurs more and more frequently. Surveys of the national trends in mean IQ's as well as studies of the effects of formal schooling and of experimental programs indicate that the margin for intellectual improvement is larger than has often been anticipated.

In a 1961 presidential address to the American Sociological Association, Robert Faris pointed out the phenomenal increase in enrollment in institutions of higher learning and how these institutions have become a "potent instrument for raising the ability level of the population". With reference to the future, he went on to say: "What is happening ... is that the nation is quietly lifting itself by its bootstraps to an importantly higher level of general ability – an achievement which, though less dramatic than a space voyage to the moon and less measurable than the Gross National Product, may mean more to the national future than either" (1961, p. 839). What effects on cognitive competence have been achieved by improved social and economic conditions related to nutrition, housing, child care and preventive medicine? The role of the welfare society is indeed to "lift" the entire population, but by doing so it also contributes to an increase in the élite which numerically needs to be increased in the post-industrial society. The long-term trend of available talent is affected by social and economic reform policies, which together provide the matrix for improved education. We can expect the average 18 to 20-year-old in Europe of the year 2000 to score at least 110 on the IQ scale of the 1960's.

We noted earlier in discussing constraints on the development of talent that there are various built-in mechanisms in the educational system which bar talent from being developed. Some of these barriers are part of the structure of the system, for instance the organizational differentiation between academic and non-academic pupils at an early age. Others are more subtle and more difficult to trace, such as grouping or teaching practices within the classroom. Some, finally, have to do with attitudes and stereotypes which discriminate between ethnic groups and sexes. Most of the constraints could be subsumed under two headings: selectivity and lack of openness. The two are evidently closely interrelated and are different aspects of the problem of flexibility as opposed to formalization, institutionalization and bureaucratization.

It has repeatedly been pointed out that the educational system as such cannot be expected to act as a "great equalizer", simply because it is there to impart competence which unavoidably means that it creates differences. But the tendency to act as a sorting agency and an allocator of social status can be either alleviated or reinforced by the adopted structure and practices. The greater the selectivity which allegedly promotes academic excellence, the more the opportunities among low status pupils to move ahead in the system are reduced. The more strict the requirements of access, promotion, examination, etc., the more biased the system is against lower class pupils.

The fundamental policy problem for most West European countries has been in the last decades and will be for the rest of this century that of organizing an educational system aimed at abolishing structural parallelism. A compulsory school for the masses and a selective secondary school essentially preparing for the university have been operating parallel to each other for a number of years. The two systems emerged from certain historical and social conditions, the compulsory elementary school being a product of the 19th century and the academic secondary school having a long tradition going back to the medieval Latin school. The latter has traditionally recruited most of its pupils from the upper social strata and prepared them for careers that confer social prestige.

Another aspect of flexibility has to do with the possibilities for a person to reenter the system once he has left it. Pupils who did not pass the "eleven-plus" examination and therefore could not enter the secondary grammar school, and pupils who dropped out of the *Gymnasium* thereby losing their chance to enter a university, are not eligible for the professional sector in the world of work. The enrollment explosion that began in recent years will rapidly create a widening "education gap" between the generations unless provisions can be made to allow adults to obtain further education which may not be directly related to their present occupations. The idea behind a system of "life-long" or "recurrent" education is to open up the institutions of higher learning, partly by waiving the formal and uniform requirements of admission and partly by tailoring the system of courses to fit *ad hoc* needs more than the requirements of package degrees.

A pervasive problem in this book – one which looms on the horizon of the post-industrial society and with which educational policy makers will have to come to grips – is the dilemma of meritocracy versus democracy. The problem can be described by stating a series of antitheses. We have on the one hand the trend toward cognitive competence becoming the "power basis", and on the other the quest for greater equality of life chances, coping power and participation. We have on the one hand the classical liberal conception of equality which entails a belief in careers being open to talent on the basis of fair competition, and on the other the radical democratic conception according to which the distribution of abilities is an arbitrary outcome of the "natural lottery". We have on the one hand the strongly felt need to improve educational opportunities for those classes who have until now been underprivileged, and on the other the immediate demands for highly trained technological and managerial manpower. We have on the one hand a strong popular demand for an "open door" policy in higher education, and on the other hand an often dominant element of competitiveness. We have on the one hand the "corrective" type of egalitarianism, according to which society should confine itself to correcting for certain differences in starting chances, such as putting all the competitors on scratch and then leaving it to individual initiative to take advantage of the equal opportunity provided; on the other there is the "redemptive" egalitarianism which emphasizes equality of results and is ready to distribute opportunities in a compensatory way. Evidently, the resolution of this dilemma is a matter of value priorities. The goal of economic growth is inextricably linked to the creation of competencies conducive to meritocracy. The goal of redemptive equality can be achieved only by playing down the rewards, status and authority connected with superior competence.

REFERENCES

ALLEN, G., K. D. PETTIGREW, L. EHLRLENMEYER-KIMLING, and S. E. STERN (1973) Heritability and Social Class: Evidence Inconclusive, *Science, 182,* 7 December, 1042–1045.

ANASTASI, ANNE (1956) Intelligence and Family Size, *Psychological Bulletin, 53,* No. 3, 187–209.

ANASTASI, ANNE (1958) *Differential Psychology,* 3rd Ed., New York: Macmillan.

ANASTASI, ANNE (1958a) Heredity, Environment, and the Question "How?", *Psychological Review, 65,* 197–208.

BAJEMA, CARL JAY (1962) Estimation of the Direction and Intensity of Natural Selection in Relation to Human Intelligence by Means of the Intrinsic Rate of Natural Increase, *Eugenics Quarterly, 9,* No. 4, 175–187.

BECKER, GARY S. (1964) *Human Capital,* New York: National Bureau of Economic Research, Columbia University Press.

BELL, DANIEL (1973) *Coming of Post-Industrial Society: A Venture in Social Forecasting,* New York: Basic Books.

BENGTSSON, JARL (1972) *Utbildningsval, utbildningsforskning och utbildningsplanering,* Lund: Studentlitteratur.

BENJAMIN, B. (1966) Social and Economic Differences in Ability, in: J. E. Meade and A. S. Parkes (Eds.), *Genetic and Environmental Factors in Human Ability,* Edinburgh: Oliver & Boyd.

BERG, IVAR (1971) *Education and Jobs: The Great Training Robbery,* Boston: Beacon Press.

BEREITER, CARL (1970) Genetics and Educability: Educational Implications of the Jensen debate, in: Jerome Hellmuth (Ed.) *Disadvantaged Child,* Vol. 3., New York: Brunner/Mazel.

BLACKBURN, JULIAN (1947) Family Size, Intelligence Score and Social Class, *Population Studies, 1,* No. 2, Sept., 1947, 165–176.

BLAU, PETER M. and OTIS DUDLEY DUNCAN (1967) *The American Occupational Structure,* New York: Wiley.

BLOOM, BENJAMIN S. et al (1971) *Handbook on Formative and Summative Evaluation of Student Learning,* New York: McGraw-Hill.

BOALT, GUNNAR (1947) *Skolutbildning och skolresultat för barn ur olika samhällsgrupper i Stockholm,* Stockholm: Norstedts.

BOUDON, RAYMOND (1973) *L'Inégalité des chances,* Paris: Armand Colin.

BOWLES, SAMUEL (1971) Cuban Education and the Revolutionary Ideology, *Harvard Educational Review, 41*, Nov. 1971, 472–500.

BOWLES, SAMUEL and HERBERT GINTIS (1973) IQ in the US Class Structure, *Social Policy, 3*, No. 4–5, 65–96.

BULCOCK, JEFFREY W., INGEMAR FÄGERLIND and INGEMAR EMANUELSSON, (1974) *Education and the Socio-economic Career: U.S. Swedish Comparisons*, Stockholm: Institute for the Study of International Problems in Education, University of Stockholm (mimeo).

BURKS, BARBARA A. (1928) The Relative Influence of Nature and Nurture Upon Mental Development, *Yearbook of the National Society for the Study of Education, 27*, Part I, Chicago: University of Chicago Press, 219–316.

BURT, CYRIL (1943) Ability and Income, *British Journal of Educational Psychology, 13*, 143, 83–98.

BURT, CYRIL (1946) *Intelligence and Fertility*, London: Hamilton.

BURT, CYRIL (1947) Family Size, Intelligence and Social Class, *Population Studies, 1*, No. 2, Sept. 1947, 177–186.

BURT, CYRIL (1966) The Genetic Determination of Differences in Intelligence: A Study of Monozygotic Twins Reared Together and Apart, *British Journal of Psychology, 57*, 1966, 137–153.

BURT, CYRIL (1969) What is Intelligence? *British Journal of Educational Psychology, 39*, 1969, 198–201.

BURT, CYRIL (1972) Inheritance of General Intelligence, *American Psychologist, 27*, No. 3, 175–190.

BUTCHER, H. J. (1968) *Human Intelligence: Its Nature and Assessment*, London: Methuen.

CATTELL, RAYMOND B. (1937) *The Fight for Our National Intelligence*, London: King.

CATTELL, RAYMOND B. (1950) The Fate of National Intelligence: Test of a Thirteen-Year Prediction, *Eugenics Review, 42*, No. 3, October 1950, 136–148.

CATTELL, RAYMOND B. (1971) The Structure of Intelligence in Relation to the Nature-Nurture Controversy, in: Robert Cancro (Ed.), *Intelligence: Genetic and Environmental Influences*, New York and London: Grune & Stratton.

CEEB College Entrance Examination Board (1960) *The Search for Talent*, College Admission No. 7. New York: College Entrance Examination Board.

COHEN, DAVID K. (1972) Does IQ Matter? *Commentary, 53*, No. 4, April 1972, 51–59.

COLEMAN, JAMES S. (1973) Effects of School on Learning: The IEA Findings, Paper presented at the IEA-Harvard Conference on Educational Achievement, November 1973, Cambridge, Mass.: Harvard Graduate School of Education (mimeo).

COLEMAN, JAMES S. *et al.* (1966) *Equality of Educational Opportunity*, Washington, D.C.: US Department of Health, Education and Welfare, Office of Education.

COMBER, L. C., and JOHN P. KEEVES (1973) *Science Education in Nineteen Countries: An Empirical Study*, with a Foreword by Torsten Husén, Stockholm: Almqvist & Wiksell; New York: Wiley.

COOK, ROBERT C. (1951) *Human Fertility: The Modern Dilemma*, New York: Sloane.

COX, C. B., and A. E. DYSON (Eds.) (1969) *Fight for Education: A Black Paper*, London: The Critical Quarterly Society, March, 1969.

CRONBACH, LEE J. (1973) Five Decades of Controversy over Mental Testing, in: Charles Frankel (Ed.), *Social Science Controversies and Public Policy Decisions*, Paper presented at a conference sponsored by the American Academy of Arts and Sciences, February 16–17, 1973.

DANIELS, NORMAN (1973) The Smart White Man's Burden, *Harper's Magazine*, October 1973, 24–40.

DOBZHANSKY, THEODOSIUS (1973) *Genetic Diversity and Human Equality*, New York: Basic Books.

DUNCAN, O. D. (1961) A Socio-economic Index for All Occupations, in: A. J. Reiss *et al.* (Eds.), *Occupations and Social Status*, Glencoe: Free Press.

ECKLAND, BRUCE K. (1967) Genetics and Sociology: A Reconsideration, *American Sociological Review*, *32*, No. 3, April 1967, 173–194.

EDMONDS, RONALD (Ed.) (1973) A Black Response to Christopher Jenck's *Inequality* and Certain Other Issues, *Harvard Educational Review*, *43*, No. 1, February 1973, 76–91.

EDMONDS, RONALD and EVELYN K. MOORE (1973) IQ, Social Class, and Educational Policy, *Change*, *5*, No. 8, October 1973, 12, 64.

EKMAN, G. (1949) Om uppskattningen av begåvningsreservens storlek, *Pedagogisk Tidskrift*, No. 7–8, 125–150.

EKMAN, G. (1951) Skolformer och begåvningsfördelning, *Pedagogisk Tidskrift*, No. 1, 15–37.

EYSENCK, H. J. (1971) *The IQ Argument: Race, Intelligence and Education*, London: Temple Smith.

EYSENCK, H. J. (1973) IQ, Social Class and Educational Policy, *Change*, No. 39, September 1973, 1–5.

FARIS, ROBERT E. L. (1961) Reflections on the Ability Dimension in Human Society, *American Sociological Review*, *26*, December 1961, 835–843.

FELDMESSER, ROBERT A. (1957) Social Status and Access to Higher Education: A Comparison of the United States and the Soviet Union, *Harvard Educational Review*, *27*, No. 2, Spring, 1957, 92–106.

FERGUSON, G. A. (1956) On Transfer and the Abilities of Man, *Canadian Journal of Psychology*, *10*, 122–131.

FINCH, F. H. (1946) *Enrollment Increases and the Changes in the Mental Level*, Applied Psychology Monographs, No. 10. Chicago: University of Chicago Press.

FLANAGAN, J. C. *et al.* (1964) *The American High School Student*. Cooperative Research Project No. 635, Washington, D.C.: United States Office of Education.

FRANKEL, CHARLES (1973) The New Egalitarianism and the Old, *Commentary*, *56*, No. 3, September 1973, 54–66.

FRASER ROBERTS, J. A., R. M. NORMAN, and R. GRIFFITHS (1938) Studies on a Child Population, *Annals of Eugenics*, London, 8, 178–215.

GAGNÉ, ROBERT M. (1968) Contributions of Learning to Human Development, *Psychological Review*, *75*, 177–191.

GALBRAITH, JOHN KENNETH (1973) *Economics and the Public Purpose*, Boston: Houghton-Mifflin.

GESSER, B., and E. FASTH (1973) *Gymnasieutbildning och social skiktning*, Stockholm: Universitetskanslersämbetet (Office of the Chancellor of the Swedish Universities).

GILLE, RENÉ, LOUIS HENRY *et al.* (1954) *Le niveau intellectuel des enfants d'âge scolaire*, La détermination des aptitudes, L'influence des facteurs constitutionels, familiaux et sociaux, Institut national d'études démographiques, Travaux et Documents, Cahier No. 23., Paris: Presses Universitaires de France.

GIRARD, ALAIN (1953) L'Orientation et la sélection des enfants d'âge scolaire dans le Département de la Seine, *Population*, No. 4, October-December, 1953.

GIRARD, ALAIN, HENRI BASTIDES, and GUY POURCHER (1963) Enquete nationale sur l'entrée en sixième et la démocratisation de l'enseignement, *Population*, No. 1, January-March 1963.

GIRARD, ALAIN, and HENRI BASTIDES (1969) Orientation et sélection;scolaire, Cinq années d'une promotion: de la fin du cycle élémentaire a l'entrée dans le 2ème cycle du second degré, *Population*, Nos. 1–2.

GRAY, J. L., and P. MOSHINSKI (1936) *The Nation's Intelligence*, London: Watts.

HALSEY, A. H. (1959) Class Differences in General Intelligence, *British Journal of Statistical Psychology, 12*, 1–4.

HALSEY, A. H. (Ed.) (1961) *Ability and Educational Opportunity*, Paris: OECD.

HANSEN, E. J. (1971) *Ungdom og uddannelse: De 14–20 åriges uddannelsesituation 1965*, Vol. II., Copenhagen: Teknisk Forlag.

HARBISON, FREDERICK H. (1973) *Human Resources as the Wealth of Nations*, London: Oxford University Press.

HARBISON, FREDERICK H., and CHARLES MYERS (1964) *Education, Manpower and Economic Growth*, New York: McGraw-Hill.

HARBISON, FREDERICK H., JOAN MARUHNIC, and JANE R. RESNICK (1970) *Quantitative Analyses of Modernization and Development*, Princeton, N.J.: Princeton University, Industrial Relations Section.

HÄRNQVIST, K. (1958) Beräkning av reserver for högre utbildning, in: *Reserverna for högre utbildning, 1955 års universitetsutredning*, Stockholm: Statens offentliga utredningar 1958: 11 (Government Printing Office).

HÄRNQVIST, K. (1959) Intelligensutveckling och skolresultat, *Pedagogisk Forskning, 2*, 57–69.

HÄRNQVIST, K. (1968) Relative Changes in Intelligence from 13 to 18, *Scandinavian Journal of Psychology, 9*, 50–82.

HECKHAUSEN, HEINZ (1973) *Leistung und Chancengleichheit*, Göttingen: Hogräfe.

VAN HEEK, FREDERICK (1968) *Het verborgen talent*, Meppel: van Gorcum.

HENRY, LOUIS (1954) L'influence des divers facteurs socio-économiques et la dimension de la famille, in: *Le niveau intellectuel des enfants d'âge scolaire*, Institut national d'études démographiques, Travaux et Documents, Cahier No. 23, Paris: Presses Universitaires de France, 47–96.

HER (1969a) *Environment, Heredity and Intelligence*, Reprint Series No. 2, Cambridge, Mass.: Harvard Educational Review.

HER (1969b) *Science, Heritability, and IQ*, Reprint Series No. 4, Cambridge, Mass.: Harvard Educational Review.

HERRNSTEIN, RICHARD (1971) IQ, *Atlantic Monthly*, *228*, No. 3, September 1971, 44–64.

HERRNSTEIN, RICHARD (1973) *IQ in the Meritocracy*, Boston and Toronto: Little, Brown & Co.

HEUYER, G., H. PIÉRON et al. (1950) *Le niveau intellectuel des enfants d'âge scolaire: Une enquête nationale dans l'enseignement primaire*, Institut national d'études démographiques, Travaux et documents, Cahier No. 13, Paris: Presses Universitaires de France.

HIGGINS, J. V., ELIZABETH W. REED, and S. C. REED (1962) Intelligence and Family Size: A Paradox Resolved, *Eugenics Quarterly*, *9*, No. 1, March 1962, 84–90.

HMSO (1954) *Early Leaving:* A Report of the Central Advisory Council for Education (England), London: Her Majesty's Stationery Office.

HÜFNER, KLAUS (Ed.) (1973) *Bildungswesen: Mangelhaft*, BRD-Bildungspolitik im OECD-Länder-examen, Frankfurt/Main: Diesterweg.

HUGHES, JOHN F., and ANNE O. HUGHES (1972) *Equal Education: A New National Strategy*, Bloomington and London: Indiana University Press.

HUNT, J. McV. (1961) *Intelligence and Experience*, New York: Ronald Press.

HUNT, J. McV. (1969) *The Challenge of Incompetence and Poverty: Papers on the Role of Early Education*, Urbana: University of Illinois Press.

HUNT, J. McV. (1973) Heredity, Environment, and Class or Ethnic Differences, in: *Assessment in a Pluralistic Society*, Proceedings of the 1972 Invitational Conference on Testing Problems, Princeton, N.J.: Educational Testing Service, 3–36.

HUSÉN, TORSTEN (1946) Intelligenskrav på olika skolutbildningsstadier, *Skola och samhälle*, *27*, 1–23.

HUSÉN, TORSTEN (1947) Begåvningsurvalet och de högre skolorna, *Folkskolan-Svensk Lärartidning*, *1*, No. 4, 124–137.

HUSÉN, TORSTEN (1948) *Begåvning och miljö*, Stockholm: Almqvist & Wiksell.

HUSÉN, TORSTEN (1950) *Testresultatens prognosvärde*, Stockholm: Almqvist & Wiksell.

HUSÉN, TORSTEN (1951a) *Begåvning och miljö*, 2nd Ed., Stockholm: Almqvist & Wiksell.

HUSÉN, TORSTEN (1951b) The Influence of Schooling upon IQ, *Theoria*, *17*, 61–88. Reprinted in: J. J. Jenkins and D. G. Paterson (1961) (Eds.), *Studies in Individual Differences in Search for Intelligence*, 677–693, New York: Appleton-Century-Crofts.

HUSÉN, TORSTEN (1953) *Tvillingstudier*, Stockholm: Almqvist & Wiksell.

HUSÉN, TORSTEN (1959) *Psychological Twin Research*, Stockholm: Almqvist & Wiksell.

HUSÉN, TORSTEN (1960) Abilities of Twins, *Scandinavian Journal of Psychology*, *1*, 125–135.

HUSÉN, TORSTEN (1961) *De farliga psykologerna*, Stockholm: Rabén och Sjögren.

HUSÉN, TORSTEN (1962) *Problems of Differentiation in Swedish Compulsory Schooling*, Stockholm: Svenska Bokförlaget–Scandinavian University Books.

HUSÉN, TORSTEN (1963) Intra-Pair Similarities in the School Achievements of Twins, *Scandinavian Journal of Psychology, 4*, 108–114.

HUSÉN, TORSTEN (1965) Curriculum Research in Sweden, *International Review of Education, 11*, No. 2, 189–208.

HUSÉN, TORSTEN (Ed.) (1967) *International Study of Achievement in Mathematics: A Comparison of Twelve Countries*, Stockholm and New York: Almqvist & Wiksell, and Wiley.

HUSÉN, TORSTEN (1968a) Life-Long Learning in the "Educative Society", *International Review of Applied Psychology, 17*, No. 2, 87–99.

HUSÉN, TORSTEN (1968b) Talent, Opportunity and Career: A Twenty-Six Year Follow-Up, *School Review, 76*, June 1968, 190–209.

HUSÉN, TORSTEN (1969) *Talent, Opportunity and Career: A Twenty-Six Year Follow-Up of 1500 Individuals*, Stockholm: Almqvist & Wiksell.

HUSÉN, TORSTEN (1971) *Present Trends and Future Developments in Education: A European Perspective*, The Peter Sandiford Memorial Lectures, Toronto: Ontario Institute for Studies in Education, Occasional Papers No. 8.

HUSÉN, TORSTEN (1972) *Social Background and Educational Career: Research Perspectives on Equality of Educational Opportunity*, Paris: OECD.

HUSÉN, TORSTEN (1973) Implications of the IEA Findings for the Philosophy of Comprehensive Education, Paper presented at the Harvard Conference on Educational Achievement, Harvard Graduate School of Education, November 1973 (mimeo).

HUSÉN, TORSTEN (1974) *The Learning Society*, London: Methuen.

HUSÉN, TORSTEN, and GUNNAR BOALT (1968) *Educational Research and Educational Change: The Case of Sweden*, Stockholm and New York: Almqvist & Wiksell, and Wiley.

HUSÉN, TORSTEN, and URBAN DAHLLÖF (1960) *Mathematics and Communication Skills in School and Society: An Empirical Approach to the Problem: of Curriculum Content*, Stockholm: Studieförbundet Näringsliv och samhälle.

HUSÉN, TORSTEN, and S. E. HENRICSON (1951) *Some Principles of Construction of Group Intelligence Tests for Adults: A Report on the Construction and Standardization of the Swedish Induction Test* (the I-Test), Stockholm: Almqvist & Wiksell.

JACKSON, BRIAN (1964) *Streaming: An Education System in Miniature*, London: Routledge and K. Paul.

JENCKS, CHRISTOPHER et al. (1972) *Inequality: A Reassessment of the Effect of Family and Schooling in America*, New York & London: Basic Books.

JENSEN, ARTHUR R. (1969) How much can we Boost IQ and Scholastic Achievement? *Harvard Educational Review, 39*, No. 1, Winter 1969, 1–123.

JENSEN, ARTHUR R. (1972) *Genetics and Education*, London: Methuen.

JENSEN, ARTHUR R. (1973) *Educability and Group Differences*, London: Methuen.

JENSEN, J., D. BERSTECHER, F. EDDING, K. HÜFNER, J. NAUMANN, and E. SCHMITZ (1972) Numerical and Systems Forecast, in: *Possible Futures of European Education*, The Hague: Nijhoff.

JOHANSSON, BROR A. (1965) *Criteria of School Readiness: Factor Structure, Predictive Value, and Environmental Influences*, Stockholm: Almqvist & Wiksell.

KAMIN, LEON (1973) Heredity, Intelligence, Politics, and Psychology, Paper presented at the Eastern Psychological Association, May 1973.

JUEL-NIELSEN, N. (1965) Individual and Environment: A Psychiatric-Psychological Investigation of Monozygous Twins Reared Apart, *Acta Psychiatrica et Neurologica Scandinavica*, Monograph Suppl. 183, Copenhagen: Munksgaard.

KARABEL, JEROME (1973) Open Admissions: Toward Meritocracy or Democracy, *Change*, No. 43, May 1972, 38–43.

KATZ, DAVID (1952) Proceedings of the 13th International Congress of Psychology in Stockholm 1951, Stockholm: Bröderna Lagerström, Boktryckare.

LASCH, CHRISTOPHER (1973) Take Me to Your Leader, *The New York Review of Books*, October 18, 1973, 63–66.

LEVIN, HENRY M. (1972) Schooling and Equality: The Social Science Objectivity Gap, *Saturday Review*, November 11, 1972, 49–51.

LINTON, RALPH (1936) *The Study of Man: An Introduction*, New York: Appleton.

LIPSET, SEYMOUR MARTIN (1972) Social Mobility and Educational Opportunity, *Public Interest*, No. 29, Fall 1972, 90–108.

MACCOBY, ELEANOR E. (Ed.) (1966) *The Development of Sex Differences*, Stanford, Calif.: Stanford University Press.

MACCOBY, ELEANOR E. and CAROL NAGY JACKLIN (1973) Sex Differences in Intellectual Functioning, in: *Assessment in a Pluralistic Society*, Proceedings of the 1972 Invitational Conference on Testing Problems, Princeton, N.J.: Educational Testing Service, 37–55.

MACHLUP, FRITZ (1962) *The Production and Distribution of Knowledge in the United States*, Princeton, N.J.: Princeton University Press.

MACHLUP, FRITZ (1973) The Growth of Knowledge Activities in the United States: Some Data gathered in connection with a Revision of "The Production and Distribution of Knowledge in the United States" (1962), Presentation at the Autumn Meeting of the US National Academy of Education.

MAXWELL, JAMES (1961) *The Level and Trend of National Intelligence: The Contribution of the Scottish Surveys*, London: University of London Press.

MOBERG, SVEN (1951) *Vem blev student och vad blev studenten?* Statistiska studier rörande fem årgångar svenska studenter under perioden 1910–1943, Lund: Gleerups.

MOBERG, SVEN, and CARL-ERIC QUENSEL (1949) *Studenternas sociala ursprung, betyg i studentexamen, vidareutbildning, yrkesval m. m.*, Stockholm: Statens offentliga utredningar 1949, No. 48 (Government Printing Office).

MOOD, ALEXANDER M. (Ed.) (1970) *Do Teachers Make a Difference?* Washington, D.C.: Department of Health, Education and Welfare, Office of Education.

MOSHINSKY, P. (1939) The Correlation between Fertility and Intelligence within Social Classes, *Sociological Review, 31*, 144–165.

MOSTELLER, FREDERICK and DANIEL P. MOYNIHAN (Eds.) (1972) *On Equality of Educational Opportunity*, New York: Vintage Books, Random House.

NEYMARK, EJNAR (1952) Universitetens och högskolornas rekryteringsreserv, in: *Vidgat tillträde till högre studier*, Stockholm: Statens offentliga utredningar. 1952, No. 29 (Government Printing Office).

NEWMAN, H. H., F. N. FREEMAN, and K. J. HOLZINGER (1937) *Twins: A Study of Heredity and Environment*, Chicago: University of Chicago Press.

OECD (1962) *Policy Conference on Economic Growth and Investment in Education*, Paris: OECD.

OECD (1965) *Reserves of Mental Abilities in the Burgenland*, Vienna: Psycho-Pedagogical Service of Austria (Mimeo).

OECD (1970) *Group Disparities in Educational Participation and Achievement*, Paris: OECD.

OECD (1971a) *Development of Higher Education 1950–1967*, Paris: OECD.

OECD (1971b) *Reviews of National Policies for Education: France*, Paris: OECD.

OECD (1971c) *Educational Policies for the 1970's*, General Report, Conference on Policies for Educational Growth, Paris, June 3rd–5th 1970, Paris: OECD.

OECD (1972) *Reviews of National Policies for Education: Germany*, Paris: OECD.

OERUM, B. (1971) *Social bakgrund, intellektuelt niveau og placering i skolesystemet*, Copenhagen: Socialforskningsinstituttet, Studie 20.

PAULSTON, ROLLAND (1968) *Educational Change in Sweden*, New York: Teachers College Press, Columbia University.

PEAKER, GILBERT F. (1974) *An Empirical Study of Education in Twenty-One Countries: A Technical Report*, Stockholm: Almqvist & Wiksell.

PEISERT, HANSGERT (1967) *Soziale Lage und Bildungschancen in Deutschland*, München: Piper.

PENROSE, L. S. (1949) The Galton Laboratory: Its Work and Aims, *Eugenics Review, 41*, No. 1, April 1949, 17–27.

PIDGEON, DOUGLAS A. (Ed.) (1967) *Achievement in Mathematics: A National Study in Secondary Schools*, London: National Foundation for Educational Research.

PLOWDEN (1967) *Children and Their Primary Schools*, A Report of the Central Advisory Council for Education (England) II: Research and Surveys, London: Her Majesty's Stationery Office.

POIGNANT, RAYMOND (1973) *Education in the Industrialised Countries*, The Hague: Nijhoff.

POSTLETHWAITE, T. NEVILLE (1967) *School Organization and Student Achievement: A Study Based on Achievement in Mathematics in Twelve Countries*, Stockholm and New York: Almqvist & Wiksell, and Wiley.

QUENSEL, C. E. (1949) Studenternas sociala rekrytering, *Statsvetenskaplig Tidskrift, 42*, Lund, Sweden, 309–322.

RAWLS, JOHN (1971) *A Theory of Justice*, Cambridge, Mass.: Harvard University Press.

REUCHLIN, MAURICE (1972) *Individual Orientation in Education*, The Hague: Nijhoff.

ROE, ANNE (1962) *The Psychology of Occupations*, 4th Printing, New York: Wiley.

ROTH, HEINRICH (Ed.) (1971) *Begabung und Lernen*, 7. Ed., Stuttgart: Klett.

SAUVY, ALFRED and GIRARD, ALAIN (1965) Les diverses classes sociales devant l'enseignement: mise au point générale des résultats, *Population*, 2e année, March-April, No. 2, 205–232.

SAUVY, A. and A. GIRARD (1970) Les diverses classes sociales devant l'enseignement, *Population et l'enseignement*, Paris: L'Institut National d'Etudes Démographiques.

SAUVY, ALFRED with the cooperation of ALAIN GIRARD, ALBERT JAQUARD and JANINA LAGNEAU-MARKIEWICZ (1973) *Access to Education: New Possibilities*, The Hague: Nijhoff.

SCARR, SANDRA (1968) Environmental Bias in Twin Studies, in: Steven G. Vandenberg (Ed.) *Progress in Human Behavior Genetics*, Baltimore, Md: The Johns Hopkins Press, 205–209.

SCARR-SALAPATEK, SANDRA (1971) Race, Social Class, and IQ, *Science, 174*, 24 December 1971, 1285–1295.

SCARR-SALAPATEK, SANDRA (1973) Heritability of IQ by Social Class, *Science*, Vol. 182, 7 December, 1045–1047.

SCOTTISH COUNCIL FOR RESEARCH IN EDUCATION (1933) *The Intelligence of Scottish Children: A National Survey of an Age Group*, London: University of London Press.

SCOTTISH COUNCIL FOR RESEARCH IN EDUCATION (1949) *The Trend of Scottish Intelligence: A Comparison of the 1947 and 1932 Surveys of the Intelligence of Eleven-Year-Old Pupils*, London: University of London Press.

SCOTTISH COUNCIL FOR RESEARCH IN EDUCATION (1953) *Social Implications of the 1947 Scottish Mental Survey*, London: University of London Press.

SENNA, CARL (Ed.) (1973) *The Fallacy of IQ*, New York: The Third Press – Joseph Okpaku Publishing Co.

SHIELDS, J. (1962) *Monozygotic Twins Brought Up Together*, London: Oxford University Press.

SHOCKLEY, WILLIAM (1972a) Dysgenics, Geneticity, Raceology: A Challenge to the Intellectual Responsibility of Educators, *Phi Delta Kappan, 53*, 297–307.

SHOCKLEY, WILLIAM (1972b) A Debate Challenge: Geneticy is 80% for White Identical Twins' IQ's, *Phi Delta Kappan, 53*, No. 7, March 1972, 415–419.

SNS (1950) *Skolreformen och näringslivet: Synpunkter på försöksverksamheten*, Stockholm: Norstedt.

SOKOLOV, J. M. (1970) Torsten Husén's Educational Points of View, *Sovjetskaja Pedagogika* (in Russian), 1970, No. 7, 126–135.

SOU (1944) *Sambandet mellan folkskolan och den högre skolan*, Stockholm: Statens offentliga utredningar, 1944, No. 21 (Government Printing Office).

SOU (1948a) *Betänkande och förslag angående studentsociala stödåtgärder*, Stockholm: Statens offentliga utredningar, 1948, No. 42 (Government Printing Office).

SOU (1948b) *Betänkande med förslag till riktlinjer för det svenska skolväsendets utveckling avgivet av 1946 års skolkommission*, Stockholm: Statens offentliga utredningar 1948, No. 27 (Government Printing Office).

SOU (1973) *Högskolan: Betänkande av 1968 års utbildningsutredning*, Stockholm: Statens offentliga utredningar, 1973, No. 2 (Government Printing Office).

SPITZ, J. C. (1962) Reserves for Higher Education in the Netherlands estimated by a Simple Method, in: *Yearbook of Education 1962*, Ed. by George Z. F. Bereday and J. A. Lauwerys, London: Evans Brothers, 481–496.

SUTHERLAND, H. E. G., and G. H. THOMSON (1926) The Correlation between Intelligence and Size of Family, *British Journal of Psychology, 17*, 81–92.

SZCZEPANSKI, JAN (1963) *Problèmes sociologiques de l'enseignement supérieur en Pologne*, Paris: Editions Anthropos.

TERMAN, LEWIS M. (1919) *The Intelligence of School Children*, Boston: Houghton-Mifflin.

THOMSON, GODFREY H. (1946) The Trend of National Intelligence, *Eugenics Review, 38*, 9–18.

THOMSON, GODFREY H. (1950) Intelligence and Fertility, *Eugenics Review, 41*, No. 4, 163–170.

THORNDIKE, ROBERT L. (1973) *Reading Comprehension Education in Fifteen Countries: An Empirical Study*, Stockholm and New York: Almqvist & Wiksell, Wiley-Halsted Press.

THUROW, LESTER C. (1972) Education and Economic Equality, *Public Interest*, Summer 1972, No. 28, 66–81.

THURSTONE, L. L. (1938) *Primary Mental Abilities*, Psychometric Monographs No. 1, Chicago: The University of Chicago Press.

TOMASSON, RICHARD F. (1965) From Elitism to Egalitarianism in Swedish Education, *Sociology of Education, 38*, No. 3, 203–223.

TROW, MARTIN (1973) Problems in Transition from Elite to Mass Higher Education, Paper presented at the Conference on Future Structures of Post-Secondary Education, Paris: OECD, June 1973 (mimeo).

TUDDENHAM, R. D. (1948) Soldier Intelligence in World Wars I and II, *American Psychologist, 3*, 54–56.

UNITED NATIONS, DEPARTMENT OF SOCIAL AFFAIRS (1955) *Proceedings of the World Population Conference in Rome, 1954*, New York: United Nations.

VANDENBERG, STEVEN G. (1966) Contributions of Twin Research to Psychology, *Psychological Bulletin, 66*, No. 5, November 1966, 327–352.

VANDENBERG, STEVEN G., RICHARD E. STAFFORD, and ANNE M. BROWN (1966) The Louisville Twin Study, in: STEVEN G. VANDENBERG (Ed.) *Progress in Human Behavior Genetics*, Baltimore, Md.: The Johns Hopkins Press, 153–204.

VERNON, PHILIP E. (1950) *The Structure of Human Abilities*, London: Methuen.

VERNON, PHILIP E. (1963) The Pool of Ability, *Sociological Review*, Monograph No. 7: Sociological Studies in British University Education. Ed. by PAUL HALMOS, Keele: University of Keele, 45–57.

WILLOUGHBY, R. R., and M. COOGAN (1940) The Correlation Between Intelligence and Fertility, *Human Biology, 12*, 114–119.

DE WOLFF, P. (1961) see HALSEY (1961).

WOLFLE, DAEL (1954) *America's Resources of Specialized Talent*, New York: Harpers.

YANOWITCH, MURRAY, and NORTON DODGE (1968) Social Class and Education: Soviet Findings and Reactions, *Comparative Education Review*, 1968, 248–267.

YOUNG, MICHAEL (1958) *The Rise of the Meritocracy*, London: Penguin.

THE AUTHOR

Torsten Husén was born in 1916. In 1944 he received his Ph.D. from the University of Lund.

He gave courses and conducted research in educational psychology in 1940's. During the 1950's and 1960's he focused his teaching and research on problems of evaluation and educational sociology. From 1953 he has been Professor of Education at the University of Stockholm, where he has held the chair in International Education since 1971.

He is also well-known abroad. He was visiting professor at, amongst others, the University of Chicago in 1959, and has twice been a Fellow at the Center for Advanced Study in the Behavioral Sciences at Stanford, in 1965–66 and 1973–74.

Professor Husén has been an adviser to the Swedish Ministry of Education and is Chairman of several international educational institutions as well as consultant to the OECD, Paris.

Professor Husén is the author of some 40 books, a number of which are mentioned in the references on pages 148-149.

INDEX